700

GREAT
RAIL-TRAILS
A National Directory

700 GREAT RAIL-TRAILS
A National Directory

Greg Smith
Karen-Lee Ryan

RAILS-TO-TRAILS CONSERVANCY

Interior layout and design by Mark A. Wood

 Printed on recycled paper

ISBN 0-925794-11-2

Manufactured in the United States of America

10 9 8 7 6 5 4 3 2 1

ACKNOWLEDGMENTS

Rails-to-Trails Conservancy is grateful to Patrick Kraich for his assistance in updating the information and maps in this book. Many thanks also go to Tom Neenan, Joe Paiva, Frank Proud, Brain Schmult and Roger Storm for their help in updating information and locating new trails in Iowa, Oregon, West Virginia, New Jersey and Michigan. Thanks to David Baslaw, Terry Berrigan, Ken Bryan, Pam Hamer, Seneca Murley, Tom Sexton and Mike Ulm for compiling the information for RTC's chapter states. Also, thanks to Caroline Baker and Leslie Sturges for fact-checking and proofreading the entire manuscript.

Finally, special thanks to all the trail managers listed in this directory who patiently responded to our detailed surveys and numerous phone calls, and who continue to provide leadership and direction to rail-trail projects across the country.

Greg Smith
Karen-Lee Ryan
August, 1995

CONTENTS

INTRODUCTION

Across America, 700 rail-trails are now open for public use. With the help of this book, you have the opportunity to embark on 700 unique journeys.

This book serves as a directory to many diverse and exciting trail experiences, such as bicycling through nearly a dozen tunnels on West Virginia's 60-mile North Bend Rail-Trail ... or hiking along the spectacular Katy Trail State Park, which parallels the Missouri River and the Lewis and Clark expedition route ... or riding horseback through the badlands and rugged canyons of the Caprock Canyons Trailway in Texas.

Explore the remains of once-thriving coal mining communities by visiting the Ghost Town Trail in Pennsylvania ... trace history along the Minuteman Bikeway outside of Boston, following the route marched by British soldiers in 1776 ... discover the scenic beauty of the Black Hills along South Dakota's George S. Mickelson Trail ... or wander along the sparkling Susan River against a backdrop of jagged canyon cliffs on Northern California's Bizz Johnson Trail.

Whether you walk, use a wheelchair, bike, skate, ride horses, cross-country ski or snowmobile, rail-trails are for you!

Because they are built on abandoned railroad corridors, rail-trails offer gentle grades and easy access for all types of recreation enthusiasts. Reflecting the booming railroad system of yesteryear, rail-trails connect urban hubs to sprawling suburbs, traverse small towns and stretch through state and national forests.

In 1916, the United States boasted the largest rail system in the world with nearly 300,000 miles of steel connecting every large city and small town in a massive transportation network.

Today, that impressive system has shrunk to less than 145,000 miles, taking a back seat to cars, trucks and airplanes. As more than 2,000 miles of track are abandoned each year, unused corridors (with tracks and ties removed) offer a perfect backbone for another type of transportation network—and a new recreation system—rail-trails.

The rail-trail movement began in the mid-1960s in the Midwest. In 1963, the late Chicago naturalist May Theilgaard Watts wrote a letter to the editor of the *Chicago Tribune* proposing constructive reuse of an abandoned right-of-way outside of Chicago.

"We are human beings," she wrote. "We are able to walk upright on two feet. We need a footpath. Right now there is a chance for Chicago and its suburbs to have a footpath, a long one." She evoked images of a trail rich in maple trees with stretches of prairie open to walkers and bicyclists.

This practical letter inspired thousands of citizens to undertake the 20-year creation of the 55-mile Illinois Prairie Path, complete with hand-built bridges, prairie remnants and wildlife-rich wetlands.

The idea spread slowly, with some of today's most well-used trails serving as cornerstones for a new movement. Wisconsin opened the Elroy Sparta Trail in 1967. Seattle cut the ribbon on the Burke-Gilman Trail in 1978. The first half of Virginia's Washington and Old Dominion Trail came into service in 1981. In 1986, when Rails-to-Trails Conservancy opened its doors and began helping communities see their dreams become reality, we knew of only 100 open rail-trails and another 90 projects in the works. Today 700 trails serve the public and nearly 1,000 additional projects are underway.

While Rails-to-Trails Conservancy does not promote the curtailment of rail-road service or the abandonment of trackage, we work to keep abandoned rights-of-way in public ownership as trails. Also, rail-trails provide a means of preserving our nation's valuable corridor system for possible future rail use.

The invaluable benefits of rail-trails speak for themselves. When the Little Miami Scenic Trail opened in southern Ohio, wheelchair-bound Sandy Stonerock traveled to the local K-Mart on her own for the first time ever. An Iowa couple initially opposed a trail project that spanned the length of their farm but completely changed their outlook after the trail was built—and even opened a bed-and-breakfast for trail users. An abandoned corridor between Baltimore and Annapolis was notorious for its vandals and open-air drug market, until the B & A Trail turned the route into the pride of the community and the most popular park in the county's system—not to mention a model rail-trail for the rest of the nation.

Every rail-trail has its own special features, and this book can help you discover and enjoy all of them. If you enjoy rail-trails, join the movement to create more trails and to save more abandoned corridors. Even a small amount of time can help build more trails.

* If you only have an hour, write a letter to your city, county or state elected official in favor of pro rail-trail legislation. You could also write a letter to the editor of your local newspaper praising a trail or trail project. Or, attend a public hearing to voice your support for a local trail.

* If you have a day, volunteer to plant flowers or trees along an existing trail or spend several hours helping out with a cleanup on a nearby rail-trail project. Or, lead a hike along an abandoned corridor with your friends.

* If you have several hours a month, become an active member in a trail effort in your area. Many rail-trail projects are completed by volunteers, and they are always looking for another helping hand.

Whatever your time allows, get involved! The success of a community's rail-trail depends upon the level of citizen participation.

The ultimate goal of Rails-to-Trails Conservancy is to help build an interconnected system of trails throughout the country. If you want to keep up on and support the movement nationally, join Rails-to-Trails Conservancy. You will get discounts on all Rails-to-Trails Conservancy publications and merchandise, and you will be supporting the largest national trails organization in the United States. To become a member, use the order form at the back of this book.

Happy Trails!
Karen-Lee Ryan
Rails-to-Trails Conservancy

HOW TO USE RAIL-TRAILS

By design, rail-trails accommodate a variety of trail users. While this is one of the many benefits of rail-trails, it also can lead to occasional conflicts among trail users. Everyone should take responsibility for ensuring trail safety by exercising caution while using rail-trails. This includes knowing the limits of your own abilities and wearing a helmet when bicycling. In addition, everyone will benefit by following a few simple trail etiquette guidelines.

One of the most basic etiquette rules is "Wheels yield to heels." Bicyclists and in-line skaters yield to all other users, while pedestrians yield to equestrians.

Generally, this means that you need to warn users (to whom you are yielding) of your presence. If, as a bicyclist, you fail to warn a walker that you are about to pass, the walker could step in front you, causing an accident that could have been prevented. Similarly, it is best to slow down and warn an equestrian of your presence. A horse can be startled by a bicycle, so make verbal contact with the rider and be sure it is safe to pass.

Here are some other guidelines you should follow to promote trail safety:
* Obey all trail-use rules posted at trailheads.
* Stay to the right except when passing
* Pass slower traffic on their left; yield to oncoming traffic when passing.
* Give a clear warning signal when passing; for example, call out "Passing on your left."
* Always look ahead and behind when passing.
* Travel at a reasonable speed.
* Keep pets on a leash.
* Do not trespass on private property.
* Move off the trail surface when stopped to allow others to pass.
* Yield to other trail users when entering and crossing the trail.
* Do not disturb any wildlife.

How To Use This Book

At the beginning of each state, you will find a map showing the general location of each rail-trail listed in that state. The text for each rail-trail includes the following information:

Trail Name: The official name of the rail-trail is stated here.

Endpoints: This heading lists the endpoints for the entire trail, usually identified by a municipality or a nearby geographical point.

Location: The county or counties through which the trail passes are stated here.

Length: This indicates the length of the trail, including how many miles currently are open, and for those trails that are built partially on abandoned corridors, the number of miles actually on the rail line.

Surface: The materials that make up the surface of the rail-trail vary from trail to trail, and this heading describes each trail's surface, which ranges from asphalt and crushed stone to the significantly more rugged original railroad ballast.

Contact: The name, address and telephone number of each trail's manager are listed here. The selected contacts generally are responsible for managing the trail and can provide additional information about the trail and its condition.

Many trail managers have maps or other descriptive brochures available free or for a small fee, and managers can also answer specific questions about their trails. If a trail is not yet fully developed, the manager can provide information about which sections are presently open and usable.

LEGEND

Every rail-trail has a series of icons depicting uses allowed on the trail.

walking, hiking, running

bicycling

mountain bikes
recommended

horseback riding

wheelchair access

in-line skating
and roller-skating

fishing access

cross-country skiing

snowmobiling

all-terrain vehicles

trail located on
a former canal

Uses permitted on individual trails are based on trail surfaces and are determined solely by trail managers. Rails-to-Trails Conservancy has no control over which uses are permitted and prohibited.

Wheelchair access is indicated for hard-surface trails. All trails that allow bicycling also allow mountain bicycling, but only on the trail surface—not in surrounding open areas. Trails that only list the mountain bicycling symbol have rougher terrains that are not suitable for road bikes. The all-terrain vehicle symbol generally does not include motorcycles and minibikes.

ALABAMA

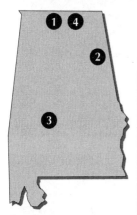

❶ Athens to Pulaski, TN

Endpoints: Athens to Pulaski, TN
Location: Giles and Limestone Counties
Length: 3.2 miles (will be 23.6 miles when completed)
Surface: Crushed stone

Contact:
Richard Martin
Athens Road Runners
P.O. Box 308
303 N. Houston Street
Athens, AL 35611-0308
(205)230-9010

❷ Chief Ladiga Trail

Endpoints: Maxwellborn to Calhoun/Cleburne County line
Location: Calhoun and Cleburne Counties
Length: 10 miles (will be 22.0 miles when completed)
Surface: Asphalt

Contact:
Tommy Allison
or Brent Morrison
City of Piedmont
109 North Center Avenue
P.O. Box 112
Piedmont, AL 36272
(205)447-9007

❸ Marion Walking Trail

Endpoints: Marion
Location: Perry County
Length: 1.0 mile
Surface: Asphalt

Contact:
Carolyn Thomas
City Clerk
City of Marion
P.O. Box 959
Marion, AL 36756
(334)683-6545

❹ Monte Sano Railway Trail

Endpoints: Monte Sano
Location: Madison County
Length: 2.0 miles
Surface: Original ballast

Contact:
Rebecca Bergquist
Huntsville Land Trust
P.O. Box 43
Huntsville, AL 35804
(205)534-5263

ALASKA

❶ Tony Knowles Coastal Bicycle Trail

Endpoints: Anchorage
Location: Anchorage County
Length: 2.5 miles of 11.0-mile trail is on abandoned rail corridor
Surface: Asphalt

Contact:
Pat Tilton
Engineering Technician
Department of Parks and Recreation
120 South Bragaw Street
P.O. Box 196650
Anchorage, AK 99501
(917)343-4474

ARIZONA

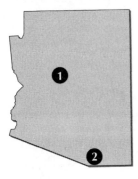

❶ Peavine Trails

Endpoints: Peavine Park
Location: Yavapai County
Length: 5.7 miles
Surface: Cinder

Contact:
Roger Pauls, Director
Chino Valley Department
of Public Works
P.O. Box 406
Chino Valley, AZ 86323-0406
(520)636-2646

❷ Railroad Trail

Endpoints:
Patagonia/Sonoita Creek
Preserve
Location: Santa Cruz
County
Length: 1.0 mile
Surface: Dirt

Contact:
Jeffrey Cooper
Preserve Manager
Patagonia-Sonoita Creek
Preserve
P.O. Box 815
Patagonia, AZ 85624-0815
(602)394-2400

ARKANSAS

❶ Marvell Bike Trail

Endpoints: Marvell
Location: Phillips County
Length: 1.3 miles
Surface: Asphalt

Contact:
City of Marvell
City Hall
P.O. Box 837
Marvell, AR 72366-0837
(501)829-2573

❷ Ozark Highlands Trail

Endpoints: Ozark-St.
Francis National Forest
Location: Crawford,
Franklin, Johnson, Newton
and Searcy Counties
Length: 2.7 miles of 155.0-
mile trail is on abandoned
rail corridor
Surface: Original ballast

Contact:
Joe Wallace
Recreation Staff Officer
Ozark-St. Francis National
Forest
P.O. Box 1008
Russellville, AR 72801
(501)968-2354

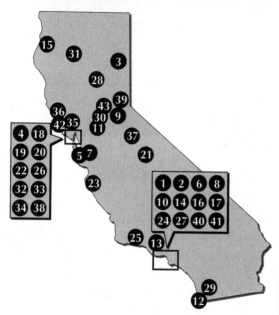

❸ Bizz Johnson Trail

Endpoints: Susanville to Westwood
Location: Lassen County
Length: 25.0 miles of 30.0-mile trail is on abandoned rail corridor
Surface: Gravel and original ballast

 on certain sections

Contacts:
Stan Bales
Outdoor Recreation Planner
Bureau of Land Management
Eagle Lake Resource Area
2950 Riverside Drive
Susanville, CA 96130
(916)257-0456

Michael Zunino
Recreation Officer
Eagle Lake Ranger District
477-050 County Road A1
Susanville, CA 96130
(916)257-4188

❶ Alton to Bristol Bike Trail

Endpoints: Santa Ana
Location: Orange County
Length: 1.5 miles
Surface: Asphalt

Contact:
Paul Johnson
Senior Parks Supervisor
City of Santa Ana
Recreation & Community Services Agency
P.O. Box 1988, M-23
Santa Ana, CA 92702-1988
(714)571-4211

❷ Atchison, Topeka and Santa Fe Trail

Endpoints: Irvine
Location: Orange County
Length: 2.5 miles
Surface: Asphalt

Contact:
Sherri Miller
Transportation Planner
E.M.A. County of Orange
P.O. Box 4048
Santa Ana, CA 92702-4048
(714)834-3137

❹ Black Diamond Mines Regional Preserve Railroad Bed Trail

Endpoints: Black Diamond Mines Regional Preserve
Location: Contra Costa County
Length: 1.0 mile
Surface: Dirt

Contact:
Steve Fiala
Trails Coordinator
East Bay Regional Park District
2950 Peralta Oaks Court
P.O. Box 5381
Oakland, CA 94605-5381
(510)635-0135

❺ Bol Park Bike Path

Endpoints: Palo Alto
Location: Santa Clara County
Length: 1.5 miles
Surface: Asphalt

Contact:
Gayle Likens
City of Palo Alto
Transportation Division
P.O. Box 10250
Palo Alto, CA 94303
(415)329-2520

❻ Bud Turner Trail

Endpoints: Fullerton
Location: Orange County
Length: 1.0 mile of 3.8-mile trail is on abandoned rail corridor
Surface: Wood chips and dirt

Contact:
Greg Meek
Engineering Department
303 W. Commonwealth Ave.
Fullerton, CA 92632-1710
(714)738-6590

❼ Creek Trail

Endpoints: San Jose
Location: Santa Clara County
Length: 1.8 miles of 2.4-mile trail is on abandoned rail corridor
Surface: Asphalt and dirt

Contact:
Mike Will, Park Ranger
Alum Rock Park
16240 Alum Rock Avenue
San Jose, CA 95132
(408)259-5477

❽ Duarte Bike Trail

Endpoints: Duarte
Location: Los Angeles County
Length: 1.6 miles
Surface: Asphalt with parallel dirt treadway

Contact:
Donna Mitzel, Director
Parks and Recreation Dept.
1600 E. Huntington Drive
Duarte, CA 91010
(818)357-7931

❾ El Dorado Trail

Endpoints: Camino to Placerville
Location: El Dorado County
Length: 2.0 miles (will be 7.0 miles when completed)
Surface: Asphalt with parallel clay treadway

Contact:
Ron Mueller, Director
Recreation and Parks
City of Placerville
549 Main Street
Placerville, CA 95667-5609
(916)642-5232

❿ Electric Avenue Median Park

Endpoints: Seal Beach
Location: Orange County
Length: 1.0 mile
Surface: Concrete and grass

Contact:
Barry Curtis
Planning Assistant
City of Seal Beach
211 8th Street
Seal Beach, CA 90740
(310)431-2527

⑪ Fairfield Linear Park

Endpoints: Fairfield
Location: Solano County
Length: 4.0 miles (will be 8.0 miles when completed)
Surface: Asphalt and concrete

Contact:
Gretchen Stranzl-McCann
Landscape Architect
City of Fairfield
1000 Webster Street
Fairfield, CA 94533
(707)428-7431

⑫ Fay Avenue Bike Path

Endpoints: San Diego to La Jolla
Location: San Diego County
Length: 0.8 miles (will be 1.0 mile when completed)
Surface: Asphalt

Contact:
Crystal Fischer
Bicycle Coordinator
City of San Diego
1222 First Avenue, MS 503
San Diego, CA 92101
(619)533-3096

⑬ Fillmore Trail

Endpoints: Fillmore
Location: Ventura County
Length: 2.0 miles
Surface: Asphalt

Contact:
Bert Rapp
City Engineer
The City of Fillmore
524 Sespe Avenue
Fillmore, CA 93015
(805)524-3701

⑭ Garden Grove to Bolsa Trail

Endpoints: Westminster
Location: Orange County
Length: 1.3 miles of 2.0-mile trail is on abandoned rail corridor
Surface: Asphalt

Contact:
Dennis Koenig
Engineering Technician
City Hall - Engineering Dept.
8200 Westminster Blvd.
Westminster, CA 92683
(714)898-3311

⑮ Hammond Trail

Endpoints: McKinleyville
Location: Humboldt County
Length: 3.0 miles (will be 5.0 miles when completed)
Surface: Asphalt and crushed stone

Contact:
Karen Suiker
Deputy Director
Humbolt County
Department of Public Works
1106 Second Street
Eureka, CA 95501-0531
(707)445-7652

⑯ Hermosa Valley Greenbelt

Endpoints: Hermosa Beach to Manhattan Beach
Location: Los Angeles County
Length: 2.0 miles
Surface: Wood chips

Contact:
Mike Flaherty
Public Works
Superintendent
City of Hermosa Beach
1315 Valley Drive
Hermosa Beach, CA 90254
(310)318-0214

⑰ Juanita Cooke Greenbelt

Endpoints: Fullerton
Location: Orange County
Length: 3.5 miles
Surface: Wood chips and dirt

Contact:
Greg Meek
Engineering Department
303 W. Commonwealth Ave.
Fullerton, CA 92632-1710
(714)738-6590

⓲ Lafayette/Moraga Trail

Endpoints: Lafayette to Moraga
Location: Contra Costa County
Length: 7.6 miles
Surface: Asphalt with parallel dirt treadway

Contact:
Steve Fiala
Trails Coordinator
East Bay Regional Park District
2950 Peralta Oaks Court
Oakland, CA 94605-5320
(510)635-0135

⓳ Lands End Trail

Endpoints: San Francisco
Location: San Francisco County
Length: 2.0 miles
Surface: Crushed stone

Contact:
Dennis Glass
Trail Crew Coordinator
Golden Gate National Recreation Area
Fort Mason Building 201
San Francisco, CA 94123
(415)556-8371

⓴ Larkspur Path

Endpoints: Larkspur to Corte Madera
Location: Marin County
Length: 1.5 miles
Surface: Asphalt

Contact:
Ben Berto
Associate Planner
Town of Corte Madera
300 Tamalpais Drive
Corte Madera, CA 94925
(415)927-5064

㉑ Merced River Trail

Endpoints: Yosemite National Park
Location: Mariposa County
Length: 8.0 miles
Surface: Original ballast and dirt

 on certain sections

Contact:
Jim Eicher
Recreation Planner
Bureau of Land Management
63 Natoma Street
Folsom, CA 95630-2671
(916)985-4474

㉒ Mill Valley–Sausalito Path

Endpoints: Mill Valley to Sausalito
Location: Marin County
Length: 3.5 miles
Surface: Asphalt with parallel crushed stone treadway

Contact:
Don Dimitratos
or Ron Miska
Parks, Open Space & Cultural Services Dept.
Marin County Civic Center
San Rafael, CA 94903
(415)499-6387

㉓ Monterey Peninsula Recreational Trail

Endpoints: Monterey to Pacific Grove
Location: Monterey County
Length: 4.3 miles
Surface: Asphalt with parallel dirt treadway

Monterey Section

Contact:
Kay Russo, Director
Monterey Recreation and Community Services
546 Dutra Street
Monterey, CA 93940
(408)646-3866

Pacific Grove Section

Contact:
John Miller, Director
Pacific Grove Recreation Department
515 Gunipero Avenue
Pacific Grove, CA 93950
(408)648-3130

㉔ Mt. Lowe Railroad Trail

Endpoints: Echo Mountain to Mt. Lowe Trail Camp
Location: Los Angeles County
Length: 4.0 miles
Surface: Original ballast and dirt

Contact:
Don Gilliland
or James Spencer
Oak Grove Ranger Station
Arroyo-Seco District
4600 Oak Grove Drive
Flint Ridge, CA 91011
(818)790-1151

㉕ Ojai Valley Trail

Endpoints: Ojai to Ventura
Location: Ventura County
Length: 9.5 miles
Surface: Asphalt with parallel wood chip treadway

Contact:
Andrew Oshita
Parks Manager
GSA Parks
800 South Victoria
Ventura, CA 93009
(805)654-3945

㉖ Old Railroad Grade

Endpoints: Mill Valley to Mt. Tamalpais State Park
Location: Marin County
Length: 9.0 miles
Surface: Original ballast and dirt

Contact:
Eric McGuire
Environmental Services Coordinator
Marin Municipal Water District
220 Nellen Avenue
Corte Madera, CA 94925
(415)924-4600

㉗ Pacific Electric Bicycle Trail

Endpoints: Santa Ana
Location: Orange County
Length: 1.6 miles
Surface: Asphalt

Contact:
Ron Ono, Design Manager
Recreation & Community Services Agency
P.O. Box 1988
Santa Ana, CA 92702
(714)571-4200

㉘ Paradise Memorial Trailway

Endpoints: Paradise
Location: Butte County
Length: 5.0 miles
Surface: Asphalt with parallel gravel treadway

Contact:
Al McGreehan
Community Development Director
Town of Paradise
5555 Skyway
Paradise, CA 95969
(916)872-6284

㉙ Rose Canyon Bicycle Path

Endpoints: San Diego
Location: San Diego County
Length: 1.3 miles
Surface: Asphalt

Contact:
Crystal Fischer
Bicycle Coordinator
City of San Diego
1222 First Avenue, MS 503
San Diego, CA 92101
(619)533-3096

㉚ Sacramento Northern Bike Trail

Endpoints: Sacramento to Rio Linda
Location: Sacramento County
Length: 8.0 miles
Surface: Asphalt

Contact:
Mike Matsuoka
Landscape Architect
Department of Public Works
1023 J Street, Room 200
Sacramento, CA 95814
(916)264-5700

㉛ Sacramento River Trail

Endpoints: Redding
Location: Shasta County
Length: 2.5 miles (will be 3.5 miles when completed)
Surface: Asphalt and concrete

Contact:
Terry Hanson
Associate Planner
City of Redding Planning Department
760 Park View
Redding, CA 96001-3318
(916)225-4030

32 San Ramon Valley Iron Horse Trail

Endpoints: Alamo to San Ramon
Location: Alameda and Contra Costa Counties
Length: 17.0 miles (will be 33.0 miles when completed)
Surface: Asphalt and concrete with parallel dirt treadway

Contact:
Steve Fiala
Trails Coordinator
East Bay Regional Park District
2950 Peralta Oaks Court
Oakland, CA 94605-5320
(510)635-0135

33 Santa Fe Greenway

Endpoints: Berkeley to Richmond
Location: Alameda and Contra Costa Counties
Length: 3.8 miles
Surface: Asphalt

Albany Section
Contact:
Jason Baker
Engineering Assistant
1000 San Pablo Avenue
Albany, CA 94706
(510)528-5760

Berkeley Section
Contact:
Jeff Egeberg, Manager
Engineering Department
2001 Addison Street
3rd floor
Berkeley, CA 94704
(510)644-6540

El Cerrito Section
Contact:
Beth Bartke
Management Assistant
City of El Cerrito
10890 San Pablo Avenue
El Cerrito, CA 94530
(510)215-4382

34 Shepard Canyon Trail

Endpoints: Oakland
Location: Alameda County
Length: 1.0 mile of 3.0-mile trail is on abandoned rail corridor
Surface: Asphalt

Contact:
Martin Matarrese
Parkland Resource Supervisor
Oakland Parks and Recreation
3590 Sanborn Drive
Oakland, CA 94602
(510)482-7857

35 Sir Francis Drake Bikeway

Endpoints: Samuel P. Taylor State Park to Tocaloma
Location: Marin County
Length: 4.5 miles
Surface: Asphalt and original ballast

Contact:
Lanny Waggoner
State Park Ranger
Samuel P. Taylor State Park
P.O. Box 251
Lagunitas, CA 94938-0251
(415)488-9897

36 Sonoma Bike Path

Endpoints: Sonoma
Location: Sonoma County
Length: 1.5 miles
Surface: Asphalt

Contact:
Patricia Wagner
Engineering Assistant
City of Sonoma
No. 1, The Plaza
Sonoma, CA 95476-9000
(707)938-3794

37 Sugarpine Railway Trail

Endpoints: Twain Harte
Location: Tuolumne County
Length: 16.5 miles (will be 30.0 miles when completed)
Surface: Gravel and dirt

Contact:
Mike Cook
Recreation Technician
Mi-Wuk Ranger District
P.O. Box 100
Mi-Wuk Village, CA 95346
(209)586-3234

38 Tiburon Linear Park

Endpoints: Tiburon
Location: Marin County
Length: 2.0 miles of 2.5-mile trail is on abandoned rail corridor
Surface: Asphalt with parallel crushed stone treadway

Contact:
Tony Iacopi, Director
Tiburon Public Works Department
1155 Tiburon Boulevard
Tiburon, CA 94920
(415)435-7899

39 Truckee River Bike Trail

Endpoints: Tahoe City to Squaw Valley
Location: Placer County
Length: 4.0 miles (will be 5.0 miles when completed)
Surface: Asphalt

Contact:
Cindy Gustafson, Director
Resource Development
Tahoe City P.U.D.
P.O. Box 33
Tahoe City, CA 96145
(916)538-3796

40 Tustin Branch Trail

Endpoints: Tustin to Villa Park
Location: Orange County
Length: 2.3 miles open in three separate sections (will be 6.0 miles when completed)
Surface: Asphalt and crushed stone

Esplanade Section
Endpoints: Tustin
Length: 0.8 miles
Surface: Crushed stone

Contact:
Sherri Miller
Transportation Planner
E.M.A. County of Orange
P.O. Box 4048
Santa Ana, CA 92702
(714)834-3137

Newport Avenue Section
Endpoints: Tustin
Length: 1.0 mile
Surface: Asphalt

Contact:
Sherri Miller
Transportation Planner
E.M.A. County of Orange
P.O. Box 4048
Santa Ana, CA 92702
(714)834-3137

Wanda Road Section
Endpoints: Villa Park
Length: 0.5 miles
Surface: Crushed stone

Contact:
Jim Konopka
Friends of the Tustin Branch Trail
P.O. Box 565
Tustin, CA 92681
(714)724-2224

41 Watts Towers Crescent Greenway

Endpoints: Los Angeles
Location: Los Angeles County
Length: 0.2 miles (will be 0.5 miles when completed)
Surface: Asphalt, crushed stone, grass and wood chips

Contact:
Dale Royal, Project Manager
Metropolitan Transportation Authority
P.O. Box 194
Los Angeles, CA 90053-0194
(213)244-6456

42 West County Trail

Endpoints: Sebastopol to Santa Rosa
Location: Sonoma County
Length: 4.0 miles (will be 11.3 miles when completed)
Surface: Asphalt with parallel dirt treadway

Contact:
Mickey Karagan
Administrative Aide
Sonoma County Regional Parks
2300 County Center Drive
Suite 120-A
Santa Rosa, CA 95403
(707)527-2041

㊸ Western States Pioneer Express Recreation Trail

Endpoints: Auburn to American River
Location: Placer County
Length: 2.0 miles of 100.0-mile trail is on abandoned rail corridor
Surface: Gravel and dirt

Contact:
Mike Lynch
Supervising Ranger
California Department of Parks and Recreation
P.O. Box 3266
Auburn, CA 95604
(916)885-4527

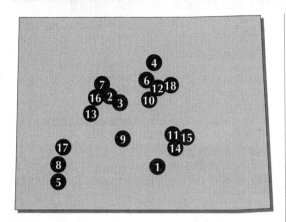

❶ Arkansas Riverwalk Trail

Endpoints: Canon City
Location: Fremont County
Length: 2.5 miles of 3.5-mile trail is on abandoned rail corridor
Surface: Crushed stone

 on certain sections

Contact:
Jeff Friesner, Manager
Canon City Metropolitan
Recreation and Park District
503 Main Street
Canon City, CO 81212
(719)275-1578

❷ Blue River Bikeway

Endpoints: Breckenridge to Dillon Reservoir (near Farmer's Korner)
Location: Summit County
Length: 3.0 miles of 6.0-mile trail is on abandoned rail corridor
Surface: Asphalt

Contact:
Scott Hobson, Manager
Open Space & Trails
Summit County Community
Development Department
P.O. Box 68
Breckenridge, CO 80424
(303)547-0681

❸ Boreas Pass

Endpoints: Breckenridge to Como
Location: Park and Summit Counties
Length: 21.7 miles
Surface: Crushed stone and gravel

Park County Section
Contact:
Sharon Kyle
Recreation Staff Officer
USFS South Park Ranger District
P.O. Box 219
Fairplay, CO 80440
(719)836-2031

Summit County Section
Contact:
Scott Hobson, Manager
Open Space & Trails
Summit County Community
Development Department
P.O. Box 68
Breckenridge, CO 80424
(303)547-0681

❹ Corridor Trail

Endpoints: Lyons
Location: Boulder County
Length: 0.5 miles of 0.8-mile trail is on abandoned rail corridor (will be 8.5 miles when completed)
Surface: Original ballast

Contact:
Kurt Carlson, Director
Parks and Recreation
Town of Lyons
P.O. Box 49
Lyons, CO 80540-0049
(303)823-6640

❺ East Fork Trail

Endpoints: San Juan National Forest
Location: Dolores County
Length: 0.5 miles of 7.5-mile trail is on abandoned rail corridor
Surface: Original ballast with parallel dirt treadway

Contact:
John Reidinger
Trails Specialist
San Juan National Forest
Dolores Ranger District
P.O. Box 210
Dolores, CO 81323-0210
(303)882-7296

❻ Fowler Trail

Endpoints: Eldorado Canyon State Park
Location: Boulder County
Length: 0.7 miles (will be 1.0 mile when completed)
Surface: Crushed stone

Contact:
Tim Metzger, Park Manager
Eldorado Canyon State Park
P.O. Box B
Eldorado Springs, CO 80025
(303)494-3943

❼ Frisco-Farmer's Korner Recreation Trail

Endpoints: Frisco to Dillon Reservoir (near Farmer's Korner)
Location: Summit County
Length: 2.5 miles (will be 8.5 miles when completed)
Surface: Asphalt

Contact:
Scott Hobson, Manager
Open Space & Trails
Summit County Community Development Department
P.O. Box 68
Breckenridge, CO 80424
(303)547-0681

❽ Galloping Goose Trail

Endpoints: Telluride to Ilium Valley
Location: San Miguel County
Length: 3 miles (will be 16 miles when completed)
Surface: Gravel and original ballast

 on certain sections

Contact:
Bill Dunkleberger
Recreation Specialist
U.S. Forest Service
Norwood Ranger District
P.O. Box 388
Norwood, CO 81423
(303)327-4261

❾ Midland Bike Trail

Endpoints: Buena Vista to Trout Creek Pass
Location: Chaffee County
Length: 6.0 miles of 12.0-mile trail is on abandoned rail corridor
Surface: Dirt

Contact:
Jeff Hyatt
Recreation Forester
Salida Ranger District
325 West Rainbow Boulevard
Salida, CO 81201
(719)539-3591

❿ Narrow Gauge Trail

Endpoints: Pine Valley Ranch Park
Location: Jefferson County
Length: 2.0 miles
Surface: Crushed stone

 on certain sections

Contact:
Mark Hearon, Trail Planner
Jefferson County Open Space
700 Jeffco Parkway, Suite 100
Golden, CO 80401
(303)271-5925

⓫ New Santa Fe Regional Trail

Endpoints: Palmer Lake to Colorado Springs
Location: El Paso County
Length: 8.0 miles of 15.0-mile trail is on abandoned rail corridor
Surface: Gravel

  on certain sections

Contact:
Susan Johnson
Supervisor of Planning
El Paso County Park Department
2002 Creek Crossing
Colorado Springs, CO 80906
(716)520-6375

⓬ Platte River Trail

Endpoints: Commerce City to Chatfield Reservoir
Location: Adams and Arapahoe Counties
Length: 2.5 miles of 28.5-mile trail is on abandoned rail corridor
Surface: Concrete

Contact:
Jed Wagner
Trails Coordinator
Denver Parks and Recreation
945 South Huron
Denver, CO 80223-2805
(303)698-4900

⓭ Rio Grande Trail

Endpoints: Woody Creek to Aspen
Location: Pitkin County
Length: 7.5 miles (will be 11.0 mile when completed)
Surface: Asphalt and gravel with parallel dirt pathway

Contact:
Patrick Duffield
Trails Supervisor
City of Aspen Parks Department
130 South Galena
Aspen, CO 81611-1902
(303)920-5120

⓮ Rock Island Trail

Endpoints: Colorado Springs
Location: El Paso County
Length: 2.7 miles (will be 6.4 miles when completed)
Surface: Asphalt

Contact:
Craig Blewitt, Senior Planner
City of Colorado Springs
Comprehensive Planning Division
Mail Code 311
P.O. Box 1575
Colorado Springs, CO 80901-1575
(719)578-6692

⓯ Shooks Run Trail

Endpoints: Colorado Springs
Location: El Paso County
Length: 1.5 miles of 1.8-mile trail is on abandoned rail corridor
Surface: Asphalt and concrete

Contact:
Craig Blewitt, Senior Planner
City of Colorado Springs
Comprehensive Planning Division
Mail Code 311
P.O. Box 1575
Colorado Springs, CO 80901-1575
(719)578-6692

⓰ Ten Mile Canyon National Recreation Trail

Endpoints: Frisco to Vail
Location: Eagle and Summit Counties
Length: 6.0 miles of 24.0-mile trail is on abandoned rail corridor
Surface: Asphalt

Eagle County Section
Contact:
Keith Montage, Planner
Eagle County Community Development
P.O. Box 179
Eagle, CO 81631-0179
(303)328-8730

Summit County Section
Contact:
Scott Hobson, Manager
Open Space & Trails
Summit County Community Development Department
P.O. Box 68
Breckenridge, CO 80424
(303)547-0681

⓱ Uncompahgre River Trail Bikepath

Endpoints: Montrose
Location: Montrose County
Length: 5.0 miles (will be 6.0 miles when completed)
Surface: Concrete

Contact:
Dennis Erickson
Parks Superintendent
City of Montrose
P.O. Box 790
Montrose, CO 81402-0790
(970)240-1481

⓲ Union Pacific Trail

Endpoints: Thornton
Location: Denver County
Length: 0.5 miles (will be 3.0 miles when completed)
Surface: Asphalt

Contact:
Lynn Lathrop
Project Analyst
Thornton Parks & Recreation Department
2211 Eppinter Boulevard
Thornton, CO 80229
(303)538-7636

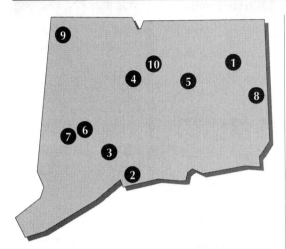

❶ Airline State Park Trail

Endpoints: Putnam to East Hampton
Location: Hartford, Middlesex, New London and Windham Counties
Length: 49.5 miles open in two separate sections
Surface: Gravel and original ballast

Northern Section
Endpoints: Putnam to Windham
Length: 26.8 miles

Contact:
John Folsom
Park Supervisor
Mashamoquet Brook
State Park
RFD 3, Wolf Den Drive
Pomfret Center, CT 06259
(203)928-6121

Southern Section
Endpoints: East Hampton to Windham
Length: 22.7 miles

Contact:
Joseph Hickey
State Park Planner
Department of
Environmental Protection
Bureau of Outdoor
Recreation
79 Elm Street
Hartford, CT 06106-1632
(203)424-3200

❷ Branford Trolley Trail

Endpoints: Branford
Location: New Haven County
Length: 1.0 mile
Surface: Crushed stone

Contact:
John Moss
Planning and Zoning Dept.
P.O. Box 150
Town Hall Drive
Branford, CT 06405
(203)488-1255

❸ Farmington Canal Linear State Park Trail

Endpoints: Cheshire to Hamden
Location: New Haven County
Length: 3 miles (will be 12 miles when completed)
Surface: Asphalt, gravel and grass

Contact:
John Thompson, Manager
Transportation Engineering
Milone & MacBroom, Inc.
716 South Main Street
Cheshire, CT 06410
(203)271-1773

❹ Farmington River Fishing Access Area

Endpoints: Collinsville to Unionville
Location: Hartford County
Length: 7.0 miles
Surface: Asphalt, crushed stone and gravel

Contact:
Daniel Dickinson
Park & Forest Supervisor
State of Connecticut
Department of Environmental Protection
178 Scott Swamp Road
Farmington, CT 06032
(203)677-1819

❺ Hop River State Park Trail

Endpoints: Manchester to Willimantic River
Location: Hartford and Tolland Counties
Length: 19.6 miles
Surface: Original ballast

Contact:
Joseph Hickey
State Park Planner
Department of Environmental Protection
Bureau of Outdoor Recreation
79 Elm Street
Hartford, CT 06106-1632
(203)424-3200

❻ Larkin Bridle Trail

Endpoints: Southbury to Hop Brook
Location: New Haven County
Length: 10.7 miles
Surface: Original ballast and cinder

Contact:
Tim O'Donoghue
Supervisor
Southford Falls State Park
175 Quaker Farms Road
Southbury, CT 06488
(203)264-5169

❼ Middlebury Greenway

Endpoints: Middlebury
Location: New Haven County
Length: 3 miles of 6-mile trail is on abandoned rail corridor
Surface: Asphalt, crushed stone and gravel

Contact:
Edward St. John
Town of Middlebury
Department of Public Works
1212 Whittemore Road
P.O. Box 392
Middlebury, CT 06762
(203)598-0614

❽ Moosup Valley State Park Trail

Endpoints: Moosup to Sterling
Location: Windham County
Length: 8.1 miles
Surface: Original ballast

Contact:
Mike Reid, Park Supervisor
Pachaug State Forest Headquarters
P.O. Box 5
Voluntown, CT 06384-0005
(203)376-4075

❾ Railroad Ramble

Endpoints: Salisbury
Location: Litchfield County
Length: 1.0 mile
Surface: Grass and dirt

Contact:
John Kaminski, Director
Salisbury Association
P.O. Box 553
24 Main Street
Salisbury, CT 06068
(203)435-0566

❿ Rockville Spur

Endpoints: Rockville
Location: Tolland County
Length: 4.1 miles
Surface: Crushed stone and dirt

 on certain sections

Contact:
Bruce Dinnie, Director
Vernon Parks and Recreation
120 South Street
Vernon, CT 06066-4404
(203)872-6118

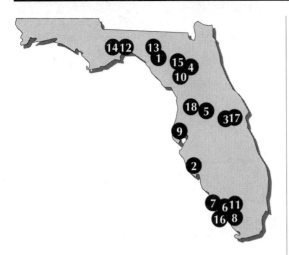

❹ Gainesville–Hawthorne State Trail

Endpoints: Hawthorne to Gainesville
Location: Alachua County
Length: 13.0 miles of 17.0-mile trail is on abandoned rail corridor
Surface: Crushed stone, original ballast and dirt

Contact:
Lisa Vidal, Ranger
Paynes Prairie State Preserve
Route 2, Box 41
Micanopy, FL 32667
(904)466-3397

❺ General James A. Van Fleet State Trail

Endpoints: Mabel to Polk City
Location: Lake, Polk and Sumter Counties
Length: 29.2 miles
Surface: Original ballast, grass and dirt

on certain sections

Contact:
Robert Seifer
Park Programs
Development Specialist
Florida Department of Environmental Protection
Division of Parks and Recreation
12549 State Park Drive
Clermont, FL 34711-8667
(904)394-2280

❶ Bell Trail

Endpoints: Bell
Location: Gilchrist County
Length: 0.8 miles
Surface: Grass and dirt

Contact:
Mark Gluckman
Town of Bell
P.O. Box 116
Bell, FL 32619
(914)463-7185

❷ Boca Grande Bike Path

Endpoints: Gasparilla Island
Location: Lee County
Length: 6.5 miles
Surface: Asphalt

Contact:
Mohsen Salehi
Transportation Planner
Lee County Department of Transportation
2022 Hendry Street
Fort Myers, FL 33901
(813)335-2220

❸ Cady Way to Fashion Square Greenway

Endpoints: Winter Park to Orlando
Location: Orange County
Length: 3.6 miles
Surface: Asphalt

Contact:
Dan Gallagher or Ben Gray
City of Orlando
Department of Public Works
400 South Orange Avenue
Orlando, FL 32801
(407)246-3395

❻ Jones Grade Trail

Endpoints: Fakahatchee Strand State Preserve
Location: Collier County
Length: 6.0 miles
Surface: Grass

Contact:
Mike Hart, Park Ranger
Fakahatchee Strand
State Preserve
P.O. Box 548
Copeland, FL 33926
(813)695-4593

❼ Mud Tram Trail

Endpoints: Fakahatchee Strand State Preserve
Location: Collier County
Length: 1.0 mile
Surface: Grass

Contact:
Mike Hart, Park Ranger
Fakahatchee Strand
State Preserve
P.O. Box 548
Copeland, FL 33926
(813)695-4593

❽ Overseas Heritage Trail

Endpoints: Key Largo to Key West
Location: Monroe County
Length: 17.5 miles open in seven sections (will be 90.0 miles when complete)

Contact:
Antonia Gerli
Bicycle/Pedestrian
Coordinator
Monroe County Planning
Department
2798 Overseas Highway
Marathon, FL 33050
(305)289-2500

Channel 5 Section
Endpoints: Fiesta Key to Craig Key
Length: 1.0 mile
Surface: Asphalt

Cudjoe Key Section
Endpoints: Cudjoe Key
Length: 2.0 miles
Surface: Dirt

Long Key to Conch Key Section
Endpoints: Long Key to Conch Key
Length: 2.3 miles
Surface: Asphalt

Lower Matecumbe Section
Endpoints: Lower Matecumbe Key
Length: 4.4 miles
Surface: Asphalt

Marathon Key to Pigeon Key Section
Endpoints: Marathon Key to Pigeon Key
Length: 2.3 miles
Surface: Asphalt

Missouri Key to Ohio Key Section
Endpoints: Missouri Key to Ohio Key
Length: 0.5 miles
Surface: Asphalt

Tom's Harbor Section
Endpoints: Grass Key to Walker's Island
Length: 5.0 miles
Surface: Asphalt and dirt

❾ Pinellas Trail

Endpoints: St. Petersburg to Tarpon Springs
Location: Pinellas County
Length: 35.0 miles
Surface: Asphalt

Contacts:
Linda Dickson
Bicycle Coordinator
Traffic & Engineering
Department
P.O. Box 490, MS 28
Gainesville, FL 32602
(904)334-2130

Carol Scherbarth
Pinellas Trail Program
Planner
Department of Planning
14 S. Ft. Harrison Ave.
Clearwater, FL 34616
(813)464-4751

❿ South Depot Avenue Bike Route

Endpoints: Gainesville
Location: Alachua County
Length: 1.0 mile (will be 2.0 miles when completed)
Surface: Asphalt

Contact:
Linda Dixon
Bicycle/Pedestrian
Coordinator
City of Gainesville, Traffic
and Engineering Department
P.O. Box 490, MS #28
Gainesville, FL 32602
(904)334-2107

⓫ South Main Trail

Endpoints: Fakahatchee Strand State Preserve
Location: Collier County
Length: 3.0 miles
Surface: Grass

Contact:
Mike Hart, Park Ranger
Fakahatchee Strand State
Preserve
P.O. Box 548
Copeland, FL 33926
(813)695-4593

⓬ Stadium Drive Bikepath

Endpoints: Tallahassee
Location: Leon County
Length: 1.5 miles
Surface: Asphalt

Contact:
Gregory Wilson
Bicycle/Pedestrian
Coordinator
Tallahassee Traffic and
Engineering Division
City Hall
Tallahassee, FL 32301
(904)891-8090

⓭ Suwannee River Greenway

Endpoints: Brandford
Location: Suwannee County
Length: 4.0 miles
Surface: Dirt

Contact:
Edwin McCook
Executive Vice President
Suwannee County
Chamber of Commerce
P.O. Drawer C
Live Oak, FL 32060
(904)362-3071

⓮ Tallahassee–St. Marks Historic Railroad State Trail

Endpoints: Tallahassee to St. Marks
Location: Leon and Wakulla Counties
Length: 15.8 miles
Surface: Asphalt with parallel dirt treadway

Contact:
Wes Smith, Park Manager
Division of Parks and
Recreation
Florida DNR,
Environmental Protection
Department
1022 Desoto Park Drive
Tallahassee, FL 32301
(904)922-6007

⑮ Waldo Road Trail

Endpoints: Gainesville
Location: Alachua County
Length: 3.0 miles
Surface: Asphalt

Contact:
Linda Dixon
Bicycle/Pedestrian
Coordinator
City of Gainesville, Traffic
and Engineering Department
P.O. Box 490, MS #28
Gainesville, FL 32602
(904)334-2107

⑯ West Main Trail

Endpoints: Fakahatchee
Strand State Preserve
Location: Collier County
Length: 3.0 miles
Surface: Grass

Contact:
Mike Hart, Park Ranger
Fakahatchee Strand
State Preserve
P.O. Box 548
Copeland, FL 33926
(813)695-4593

⑰ West Orange Trail

Endpoints: Wintergarden
to Orange County line
Location: Orange County
Length: 5 miles (will be 20
miles when completed)
Surface: Asphalt

  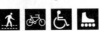

Contact:
Brook Sealle, Supervisor
West Orange Trail, County
Line Station
17922 Old County Road 50
Wintergarden, FL 34787
(407)656-2509

⑱ Withlacoochee State Trail

Endpoints: Citrus Springs
to Dade City
Location: Citrus,
Hernando and Pasco
Counties
Length: 46.0 miles
Surface: Asphalt with
parallel dirt treadway

Contact:
Robert Seifer
Park Programs
Development Specialist
Florida Department of
Environmental Protection
Division of Parks &
Recreation
12549 State Park Drive
Clermont, FL 34711-8667
(904)394-2280

❶ Augusta Canal Trail

Endpoints: Headgates to Turning Basin
Location: Richmond County
Length: 7.0 miles
Surface: Dirt

Contact:
Thomas Robertson
Augusta Canal Authority
P.O. Drawer 2546
Augusta, GA 30903
(706)722-1071

❷ Chatahoochee Trail

Endpoints: Columbus to Ft. Benning
Location: Muscogee County
Length: 1 mile (will be 11.5 miles when completed)
Surface: Asphalt

Contact:
Rick Gordon, Director
Columbus Parks and
Recreation Dept.
P.O. Box 1340
Columbus, GA 31902-1340
(706)571-4785

❸ Heritage Park Trail

Endpoints: Rome
Location: Floyd County
Length: 4.0 miles
Surface: Asphalt and grass

Contact:
Tim Banks
Assistant Director
Rome-Floyd Parks &
Recreation Authority
300 West Third Street
Rome, GA 30165-2803
(706)291-0766

❹ Old Savannah-Tybee RR Historic & Scenic Multipurpose Trail

Endpoints: Savannah
Location: Chatham County
Length: 6.5 miles
Surface: Crushed stone and dirt

 on certain sections

Contact:
Jim Golden, Director
Chatham County Parks &
Recreation Department
P.O. Box 1746
Savannah, GA 31402
(912)652-6780

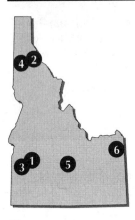

❶ Greenbelt Trail

Endpoints: Lucky Peak Reservoir to Boise
Location: Ada County
Length: 5.0 miles of 12.0-mile trail is on abandoned rail corridor
Surface: Asphalt

Contact:
Donna Griffin
Parks & Waterways Director
Ada County Parks & Recreation
650 Main Street
Boise, ID 83702
(208)343-1328

❷ Mullan Pass–Lookout Pass Loop

Endpoints: Lookout Pass to Mullan
Location: Shoshone County
Length: 8.0 miles
Surface: Original ballast

Contact:
Steve Williams
District Ranger
Idaho Panhandle National Forest
P.O. Box 14
Silverton, ID 83867
(208)752-1221

❸ Nampa to Stoddard

Endpoints: Nampa to Stoddard
Location: Canyon County
Length: 1.5 miles (will be 16.9 miles when completed)
Surface: Gravel

Contact:
Larry Bledsoe, Director
Nampa Engineering Dept.
411 Third Street South
Nampa, ID 83651
(208)466-2220

❹ North Idaho Centennial Trail

Endpoints: Coeur d'Alene to Idaho state line
Location: Kootenai County
Length: 5.0 miles of 18.0-mile trail is on abandoned rail corridor
Surface: Asphalt

Contact:
Bob MacDonald
Kootenai County Commissioner
Coeur d'Alene, ID 83816
(208)769-4450

❺ Wood River Trails

Endpoints: Ketchum to Bellevue
Location: Blaine County
Length: 10.0 miles of 22.0-mile trail is on abandoned rail corridor
Surface: Asphalt with parallel wood chip treadway

Contact:
Mary Austin Crofts, Director
Blaine County Recreation District
P.O. Box 297
Hailey, ID 83333-0297
(208)788-2117

❻ Yellowstone Branch Line Trail

Endpoints: Warm River to Montana state line
Location: Fremont County
Length: 34.0 miles
Surface: Original ballast

Contact:
Bart Andreasen
Landscape Architect
420 North Bridge Street
P.O. Box 208
St. Anthony, ID 83445
(208)624-3151

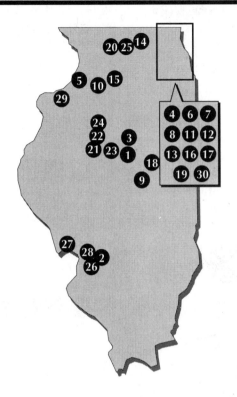

❸ El Paso Trail

Endpoints: El Paso
Location: Woodford County
Length: 2.7 miles
Surface: Crushed stone

Contact:
Ted Gresham, Administrator
Town of El Paso
City Hall
52 North Elm
El Paso, IL 61738-1545
(309)527-4005

❹ Fox River Trail

Endpoints: Aurora to Crystal Lake
Location: Kane and McHenry Counties
Length: 33.0 miles
Surface: Asphalt and crushed stone

Contacts:
Bill Donnell
Landscape Architect
Fox Valley Park District
712 South River Street
Aurora, IL 60506
(708)897-0516

Jon Duerr
Director of Field Services
Kane County Forest Preserve
719 Batavia Avenue
Building G
Geneva, IL 60134
(708)232-5981

❶ Constitution Trail

Endpoints: Bloomington to Normal
Location: McLean County
Length: 5.3 miles
Surface: Asphalt

Contact:
Keith Rich, Director
Bloomington Parks and Recreation Department
109 East Olive Street
Bloomington, IL 61701
(309)823-4260

❷ Delyte Morris Bikeway

Endpoints: Edwardsville
Location: Madison County
Length: 2.6 miles
Surface: Crushed stone

Contact:
Anna Schonlau
Assistant Recreation Director
Southern Illinois University at Edwardsville
Recreation Department
P.O. Box 1057
Edwardsville, IL 62026
(618)692-3235

❺ Great River Trail

Endpoints: Rock Island to Savanna
Location: Carroll, Rock Island and Whiteside Counties
Length: 28 miles (will be 62 miles when completed)
Surface: Asphalt and crushed stone

Contact:
Patrick Marsh
Bikeway Coordinator
Bi-State Regional
Commission
1504 Third Avenue
Rock Island, IL 61201
(309)793-6300

❻ Great Western Trail

Endpoints: St. Charles to Sycamore
Location: DeKalb and Kane Counties
Length: 18.0 miles
Surface: Asphalt and crushed stone

DeKalb County Section
Contact:
Terry Hannan
Superintendent
DeKalb County Forest
Preserve
110 E. Sycamore Street
Sycamore, IL 60178
(815)895-7191

Kane County Section
Contact:
Jon Duerr
Director of Field Services
Kane County Forest
Preserve
719 Batavia Avenue
Geneva, IL 60134-3077
(708)232-5981

❼ Great Western Trail (Dupage Parkway Section)

Endpoints: Villa Park
Location: DuPage County
Length: 12.0 miles
Surface: Crushed stone

Contact:
Charles Tokarski
County Engineer
DuPage County DOT
130 N. County Farm Road
Wheaton, IL 60189
(708)682-7318

❽ Green Bay Trail

Endpoints: Highland Park to Wilmette
Location: Cook and Lake Counties
Length: 9.5 miles
Surface: Asphalt and crushed stone

Glencoe Section

Contact:
John Houde
Community Development
Head
Village of Glencoe
675 Village Court
Glencoe, IL 60022-1639
(708)835-4111

Highland Park Section

Contact:
Larry King, Superintendent
Highland Park Forestry Dept.
1150 Half Day Road
Highland Park, IL 60035
(708)432-0800

Wilmette Section

Contact:
Bill Lambrecht
Wilmette Park District
1200 Wilmette Ave
Wilmette, IL 60091-2793
(708)256-6100

Winnetka Section

Contact:
Dan Newport, Director
Winnetka Park District
520 Glendale Road, Suite 200
Winnetka, IL 60093-2552
(708)501-2040

❾ Heartland Pathways

Endpoints: Seymour to Clinton & Cisco
Location: Champaign, De Witt and Piatt Counties
Length: 33 miles (will be 40 miles when completed)
Surface: Original ballast

Contact:
David Monk, President
Heartland Pathways
115 North Market Street
Champaign, IL 61820-4004
(217)351-1911

⑩ Hennepin Canal Parkway

Location: Bureau, Henry, Lee and Whiteside Counties
Length: 96.0 miles open in two sections
Surface: Crushed stone and grass

Contact:
Steve Moser
Site Superintendent
Illinois Department of Natural Resources
Hennepin Canal Parkway
RR 2, Box 201
Sheffield, IL 61361
(815)454-2328

Atkinson Section

Endpoints: Lock 30 to Lock 32 (near Atkinson)
Length: 5.0 miles
Surface: Crushed stone

Bureau Junction to Atkinson Section

Endpoints: Bureau Junction to Atkinson with spur to Rock Falls
Length: 91.0 miles
Surface: Crushed stone and grass

 on certain sections

⑪ Illinois & Michigan Canal National Heritage Corridor

Endpoints: Joliet to La Salle
Location: DuPage, Grundy, La Salle and Will Counties
Length: 68.5 miles open in five sections (will be 85.0 miles when completed)
Surface: Asphalt and gravel

Contact:
Vincent Michael
Centennial Trail
Associate Director
Canal Corridor Association
220 South State Street
Suite 1880
Chicago, IL 60604
(312)427-3688

Centennial Trail Section

Endpoints: Lemont to Romeoville
Length: 3.5 miles (will be 20 miles when completed)
Surface: Gravel

Joliet to La Salle Section

Endpoints: Joliet to La Salle
Length: 55.0 miles
Surface: Gravel

Lemont Section

Endpoints: Lemont
Length: 2.5 miles
Surface: Gravel

Lockport Section

Endpoints: Lockport
Length: 2.5 miles
Surface: Gravel

Sag Bridge to Willow Springs Section

Endpoints: Sag Bridge to Willow Springs
Length: 5.0 miles
Surface: Asphalt

⑫ Illinois Prairie Path

Endpoints: Maywood to Wheaton with spurs to Aurora, Batavia, Elgin & Geneva
Location: Cook, DuPage and Kane Counties
Length: 55.0 miles
Surface: Crushed stone and dirt

Contacts:
Bill Donnell
Landscape Architect
Fox Valley Park District
P.O. Box 818
Aurora, IL 60507
(708)897-0516

Ruth Karupensky
Principal Planner
DuPage County DOT
130 N. County Farm Road
Wheaton, IL 60189
(708)682-7318

⓭ Libertyville Trail

Endpoints: Libertyville
Location: Lake County
Length: 3.0 miles
Surface: Crushed stone

Contact:
Steve Magnusen
Director of Public Works
200 East Cook Avenue
Libertyville, IL 60048-2090
(708)362-2430

⓮ Long Prairie Trail

Endpoints: Poplar Grove
to McHenry County line
Location: Boone County
Length: 11 miles (will be
12.5 miles when completed)
Surface: Asphalt

Contact:
John Kremer
Executive Director
Boone County
Conservation District
7600 Appleton Road
Belvidere, IL 61008
(815)547-7935

⓯ Lowell Parkway Bicycle Path

Endpoints: Dixon
Location: Lee County
Length: 2.9 miles of 3.1-
mile trail is on abandoned
rail corridor
Surface: Asphalt

Contact:
Dave Zinnen
Director of Administration
and Recreation
Dixon Park District
804 Palmyra Avenue
Dixon, IL 61021-1960
(815)284-3306

⓰ McHenry County Prairie Trail

Location: McHenry
County
Length: 12.0 miles open in
two separate sections

Northern Section

Endpoints: Ringwood to
Wisconsin state line
Length: 7.5 miles
Surface: Gravel and origi-
nal ballast

 on certain
sections

Contact:
Mary Eysenbach
Assistant Director
McHenry County
Conservation District
6512 Harts Road
Ringwood, IL 60072
(815)678-4431

Southern Section

Endpoints: Crystal Lake to
Kane County line
Length: 4.5 miles
Surface: Asphalt

Contact:
Steve Weller
Executive Director
McHenry County
Conservation Dist
6512 Harts Road
Ringwood, IL 60072
(815)678-4361

⓱ North Shore Path

Endpoints: Winthrop
Harbor to Mundelein
Location: Lake County
Length: 18.9 miles of 21.2-
mile trail is on abandoned
rail corridor
Surface: Crushed stone

Contact:
Martin Buehler
or Edward Nelson
Lake County Division of
Transportation
600 West Winchester Road
Libertyville, IL 60048
(708)362-3950

⓲ O'Malley's Alley

Endpoints: Champaign
Location: Champaign
County
Length: 0.5 miles
Surface: Concrete

Contact:
James Spencer
Director of Operations
Champaign Park District
706 Kenwood Drive
Champaign, IL 61821-4112
(217)398-2550

⓲ Palatine Trail

Endpoints: Palatine
Location: Cook County
Length: 1.0 mile of 28.0-mile trail is on abandoned rail corridor
Surface: Asphalt

Contact:
Cheryl Scensay
Landscape Architect
Palatine Park District
250 East Wood Street
Palatine, IL 60067
(708)705-5140

⓴ Pecatonica Prairie Path

Endpoints: Freeport to Rockford
Location: Stephenson and Winnebago Counties
Length: 20.0 miles
Surface: Original ballast

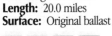

Contact:
Rick Strader
Manager of Planning & Development
Rockford Park District
1401 North Second Street
Rockford, IL 61107
(815)987-8856

㉑ Pimiteoui Bike Trail

Endpoints: Peoria
Location: Peoria County
Length: 1.7 miles (will be 4.2 miles when completed)
Surface: Asphalt

Contact:
Peoria Park District
2218 N. Prospect Road
Peoria, IL 61603
(309)682-1200

㉒ Pioneer Parkway

Endpoints: Peoria to Alta
Location: Peoria County
Length: 2.5 miles
Surface: Crushed stone

Contact:
Peoria Park District
2218 N. Prospect Road
Peoria, IL 61603
(309)682-1200

㉓ River Trail of Illinois

Endpoints: East Peoria to Morton
Location: Tazewell County
Length: 7 miles (will be 14 miles when completed)
Surface: Asphalt

Contact:
Jim Coutts or Brad Smith
Fondulac Park District
201 Veterans Drive
East Peoria, IL 61611
(309)699-3923

㉔ Rock Island Trail State Park

Endpoints: Alta to Toulon
Location: Peoria and Stark Counties
Length: 28.3 miles
Surface: Crushed stone

Contact:
Paul Oltman, Trail Ranger
Rock Island Trail State Park
P.O. Box 64
Wyoming, IL 61491-0064
(309)695-2228

㉕ Rock River Recreation Path

Endpoints: Rockford to Love's Park
Location: Winnebago County
Length: 2.0 miles of 3.3-mile trail is on abandoned rail corridor
Surface: Asphalt

Contact:
Vance Barrie
Marketing Coordinator
Rockford Park District
1401 North Second Street
Rockford, IL 61107
(815)987-8694

㉖ Ronald J. Foster Heritage Trail

Endpoints: Glen Carbon
Location: Madison County
Length: 3.2 miles
Surface: Asphalt

Contact:
Glen Carbon Village Hall
P.O. Box 757
151 North Main Street
Glen Carbon, IL 62034
(618)288-1200

㉗ Sam Vadalabene Great River Road Bike Trail

Endpoints: Alton to Grafton
Location: Jersey and Madison Counties
Length: 5.5 miles of 14.0-mile trail is on abandoned rail corridor
Surface: Asphalt

Contact:
Ronald Tedesco
District Bikeway Coordinator
Illinois Department of Transportation
1100 Eastport Plaza Drive
P.O. Box 988
Collinsville, IL 62234
(618)346-3100

㉘ Vadalabene Nature Trail

Endpoints: Edwardsville to Long Lake
Location: Madison County
Length: 6.3 miles (will be 10.3 miles when completed)
Surface: Original ballast

Contact:
George Arnold
Madison County Trail Volunteers
1306 St. Louis Street
Edwardsville, IL 62025-1310
(618)656-7195

㉙ Village Bike Path

Endpoints: Northbrook
Location: Cook County
Length: 0.5 miles
Surface: Asphalt

Contact:
Edward Harvey
Superintendent of Parks & Property
Northbrook Park District
1720 Pfingsten Street
Northbrook, IL 60062-5850
(708)291-2960

㉚ Virgil Gilman Nature Trail

Endpoints: Blisswoods Forest Preserve to Montgomery
Location: Kane County
Length: 14.0 miles
Surface: Asphalt and crushed stone

Contact:
Bill Donnell
Landscape Architect
Fox Valley Park District
P.O. Box 818
Aurora, IL 60507
(708)897-0516

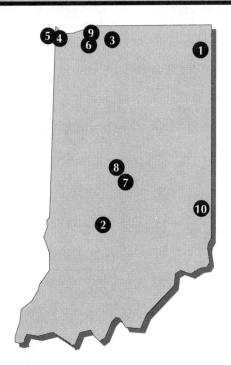

❸ East Bank Trail

Endpoints: South Bend to Roseland
Location: St. Joseph County
Length: 0.5 miles (will be 7.5 miles when completed)
Surface: Asphalt

Contact:
Betsy Harriman
South Bend Parks Dept.
301 S. St. Louis Boulevard
South Bend, IN 46617
(219)235-9401

❹ Erie Trail Linear Park

Endpoints: Downtown Hammond to Little Calumet River
Location: Lake County
Length: 4.7 miles
Surface: Asphalt

Contact:
Kathy Kazmierczak
Special Events Coordinator
Hammond Park Dept.
5825 Sohl Avenue
Hammond, IN 46320
(219)853-6378

❶ Auburn to Waterloo Bike Trail

Endpoints: Auburn to Waterloo
Location: DeKalb County
Length: 4.0 miles
Surface: Concrete

Contact:
Andy Jagoda
Superintendent
Auburn Parks Department
P.O. Box 506
Auburn, IN 46706-0506
(219)925-8245

❷ Clear Creek Rail Trail

Endpoints: Bloomington to Victor
Location: Monroe County
Length: 4.0 miles (will be 7.0 miles when completed)
Surface: Original ballast

Contact:
Leslie Clark
Cultural/Outdoor Recreation Director
Bloomington Parks & Recreation
349 South Walnut Street
Bloomington, IN 47401-3511
(812)349-3700

❺ Hammond Linear Trail

Endpoints: Hammond
Location: Lake County
Length: 4.0 miles (will be 4.3 miles when completed)
Surface: Asphalt

Contact:
Pat Moore, Administrator
Hammond Park Dept.
601 Conkey Street
Hammond, IN 46320
(219)853-6436

❻ Iron Horse Heritage Trail

Endpoints: Portage
Location: Porter County
Length: 5.0 miles
Surface: Gravel

Contact:
Carl Fisher, Superintendent
City of Portage Parks &
Recreation Department
2100 Willowcreek Road
Portage, IN 46368
(219)762-1675

❼ Monon Trail

Endpoints: Indianapolis
Location: Marion County
Length: 2.0 miles (will be 8.0 miles when completed)
Surface: Asphalt, crushed stone and dirt

Contact:
Ray Irvin
Indianapolis Greenways
1426 W. 29th Street
Indianapolis, IN 46208-4945
(317)924-7431

❽ Nancy Burton Memorial Trail

Endpoints: Zionsville
Location: Boone County
Length: 2.1 miles
Surface: Original ballast

Contact:
David Brown
Zionsville Town Council
6 North Elm Street
Zionsville, IN 46077-1542
(317)873-6024

❾ Prairie–Duneland Trail

Endpoints: Portage
Location: Lake and Porter Counties
Length: 6 miles (will be 28 miles when completed)
Surface: Asphalt

Contact:
Carl Fisher, Superintendent
City of Portage Parks &
Recreation Department
2100 Willowcreek Road
Portage, IN 46368
(219)762-1675

❿ Whitewater Canal Trail

Endpoints: Brookville to Metamora
Location: Franklin County
Length: 2.0 miles (will be 8.0 miles when completed)
Surface: Dirt

Contact:
Mike Martin
Streams & Trails Specialist
Indiana Department of
Natural Resources
402 West Washington,
Room 271
Indianapolis, IN 46204
(317)232-4070

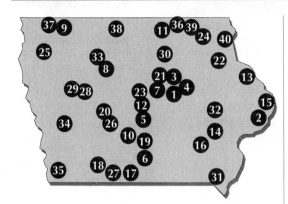

❶ Benton Preserve Trail

Endpoints: Atkins
Location: Benton County
Length: 1.0 mile
Surface: Original ballast

Contact:
Kevin Kasena
Benton County
Conservation Board
2113 57th Street
Vinton, IA 52349
(319)472-4942

❷ Brookfield Wildlife Refuge Trail

Endpoints: Brookfield
Wildlife Refuge
Location: Clinton County
Length: 2.0 miles
Surface: Grass and dirt

Contact:
Al Griffith, Director
Clinton County
Conservation Board
P.O. Box 161
Grand Mound, IA 52751
(319)847-7202

❸ Cedar Prairie Trail

Endpoints: Cedar Falls
Location: Black Hawk
County
Length: 1 mile of 4.5-mile
trail is on abandoned rail
corridor
Surface: Concrete

Contact:
Dick Bruns
Park Division Manager
Cedar Falls Parks Division
606 Union Road
Cedar Falls, IA 50613-1666
(319)273-8625

❹ Cedar Valley Nature Trail

Endpoints: Hiawatha to
Evansdale
Location: Benton, Black
Hawk, Buchanan and Linn
Counties
Length: 52.0 miles of 53.0-
mile trail is on abandoned
rail corridor
Surface: Crushed stone

Black Hawk and Buchanan County Sections

Contact:
Steve Finegan
Executive Director
Black Hawk County
Conservation Board
2410 West Lone Tree Road
Cedar Falls, IA 50613-1093
(319)277-1536

Linn and Benton County Sections

Contact:
Dennis Goemaat
Deputy Director
Linn County Conservation
Board
1890 County Home Road
Marion, IA 52302
(319)398-3505

❺ Chichaqua Valley Trail

Endpoints: Bondurant to Baxter
Location: Jasper and Polk Counties
Length: 21.0 miles
Surface: Crushed stone and original ballast

Jasper County Section

Contact:
John Parsons, Parks Officer
Jasper County
Conservation Board
115 North Second Avenue
Newton, IA 50208
(515)792-9780

Polk County Section

Contact:
Ben Van Grundy, Director
Polk County Conservation Board
Jester Park
Granger, IA 50109
(515)999-2557

❻ Cinder Path

Endpoints: Chariton to Lucas-Wayne County line
Location: Lucas and Wayne Counties
Length: 13.5 miles
Surface: Original ballast

Contact:
Dwayne Clanin, Supervisor
P.O. Box 78
Chariton, IA 50049-0078
(515)774-2314

❼ Comet Trail

Endpoints: Conrad to Wolf Creek Park
Location: Grundy County
Length: 4.0 miles (will be 6.3 miles when completed)
Surface: Crushed stone and grass

Contact:
Kevin Williams, Director
Grundy County
Conservation Board
P.O. Box 36
Morrison, IA 50657
(319)345-2688

❽ Fort Dodge Nature Trail

Endpoints: Fort Dodge
Location: Webster County
Length: 3.0 miles
Surface: Crushed stone and gravel

Contact:
Michael Norris, City Forester
Department of Parks, Recreation and Forestry
813 First Avenue South
Fort Dodge, IA 50501-4725
(515)573-5791

❾ Great Lakes Spine Trail

Endpoints: Milford to Spirit Lake
Location: Dickinson County
Length: 6.0 miles of 10.5-mile trail is on abandoned rail corridor
Surface: Asphalt

Contact:
John Walters, Director
Dickinson County
Conservation Board
1924 240th Street
Milford, IA 51351-1376
(712)338-4786

⑩ Great Western Trail

Endpoints: Des Moines to Martinsdale
Location: Polk and Warren Counties
Length: 18.2 miles
Surface: Asphalt and crushed stone

Polk County Section
Contact:
Ben Van Grundy, Director
Polk County Conservation Board
Jester Park
Granger, IA 50109
(515)999-2557

Warren County Section
Contact:
Jim Priebe, Director
Warren County Conservation Board
1565 118th Avenue
Indianola, IA 50125-9005
(515)961-6169

⑪ Harry Cook Nature Trail

Endpoints: Osage to Spring Park
Location: Mitchell County
Length: 1.5 miles of 2.0-mile trail is on abandoned rail corridor
Surface: Crushed stone and gravel

Contact:
Ted Funk, Director
Parks and Recreation
114 South 7th Street
City Hall
Osage, IA 50461
(515)732-3709

⑫ Heart of Iowa Nature Trail

Endpoints: Melbourne to Slater
Location: Marshall and Story Counties
Length: 26.0 miles of 32.0-mile trail is on abandoned rail corridor
Surface: Crushed stone with parallel grass treadway

Contact:
Steven Lekwa
Deputy Director
McFarland Park
RR 2, Box 272 E
Ames, IA 50010-9651
(515)232-2516

⑬ Heritage Trail

Endpoints: Dubuque to Dyersville
Location: Dubuque County
Length: 27 miles (will be 30 miles when completed)
Surface: Crushed stone

Contacts:
Robert Walton
or Carol Freund
Dubuque County Conservation Board
13768 Swiss Valley Road
Peosta, IA 52068
(319)556-6745

⑭ Hoover Nature Trail

Endpoints: Cedar Rapids to Burlington
Location: Cedar, Des Moines, Johnson, Muscatine, Linn and Louisa Counties
Length: 23 miles (will be 115 miles when completed)
Surface: Crushed stone and original ballast with a parallel dirt treadway

 on certain sections

Contact:
Millie Gregg
Executive Director
Hoover Nature Trail, Inc.
P.O. Box 123
West Liberty, IA 52776-0123
(319)627-2626

⑮ Jackson County Trail

Endpoints: Spragueville
Location: Jackson County
Length: 3.3 miles of 3.8-mile trail is on abandoned rail corridor
Surface: Crushed stone

Contact:
Ann Burns
Jackson County Conservation Board
201 West Platt Road
Maquoketa, IA 52060
(319)652-3783

⑯ Kewash Nature Trail

Endpoints: Keota to Washington
Location: Washington County
Length: 13.0 miles
Surface: Crushed stone

Contact:
Washington County
Conservation Board
P.O. Box 889
Washington, IA 52353-0889
(319)653-7765

⑰ Little River Nature Trail

Endpoints: Leon
Location: Decatur County
Length: 0.9 miles of 2.0-mile trail is on abandoned rail corridor
Surface: Concrete

Contacts:
Carolyn Carroll, City Clerk
City Hall
104 West First Street
Leon, IA 50144
(515)446-6221

Rick Erke
Conservationist
RR #1
Leon, IA 50144
(515)446-7307

⑱ Maple Leaf Pathway

Endpoints: Diagonal
Location: Ringgold County
Length: 2.5 miles
Surface: Crushed stone and grass

Contact:
Rick Hawkins, Director
Ringgold County
Conservation Board
P.O. Box 83A, RR 1
Mount Ayr, IA 50854
(515)464-2787

⑲ McVay Trail

Endpoints: Indianola
Location: Warren County
Length: 1.4 miles of 1.6-mile trail is on abandoned rail corridor
Surface: Asphalt

Contact:
Glenn Cowan, Director
Indianola Parks &
Recreation Department
110 North First Street
Indianola, IA 50125-2527
(515)961-9420

⑳ Perry to Rippey Trail

Endpoints: Perry to Rippey
Location: Boone, Dallas and Greene Counties
Length: 9.0 miles
Surface: Original ballast and dirt

Boone County Section
Contact:
Tom Foster, Director
Boone County
Conservation Board
610 H Avenue
Ogden, IA 50212
(515)353-4237

Dallas County Section
Contact:
Jeff Logsdon, Director
Dallas County Conservation Board
1477 K Avenue
Perry, IA 50220
(515)465-3577

Greene County Section
Contact:
Dan Towers, Director
Greene County
Conservation Board
Courthouse
Jefferson, IA 50129
(515)386-4629

㉑ Pioneer Trail

Endpoints: Reinbeck to Holland
Location: Grundy County
Length: 9.0 miles of 12.0-mile trail is on abandoned rail corridor
Surface: Crushed stone with parallel grass treadway

Contact:
Kevin Williams, Director
Grundy County
Conservation Board
P.O. Box 36
Morrison, IA 50657
(319)345-2688

㉒ Pony Hollow Trail

Endpoints: Elkader
Location: Clayton County
Length: 4.0 miles
Surface: Crushed stone

Contact:
Don Menken, Director
Clayton County
Conservation Board
RR 2, Box 65A
Elkader, IA 52043-9524
(319)245-1516

㉓ Praeri Rail Trail

Endpoints: Roland to Zearing
Location: Story County
Length: 10.5 miles
Surface: Crushed stone, grass and dirt

Contact:
Steven Lekwa
Deputy Director
McFarland Park
RR 2, Box 272 E
Ames, IA 50010-9651
(515)232-2516

㉔ Prairie Farmer Recreational Trail

Endpoints: Calmar to Cresco
Location: Winneshiek County
Length: 17.5 miles of 18.2-mile trail is on abandoned rail corridor
Surface: Crushed stone

Contact:
David Oestmann, Director
Winneshiek County
Conservation Board
2546 Lake Meyer Road
Fort Atkinson, IA 52144
(319)534-7145

㉕ Puddle Jumper Trail

Endpoints: Orange City to Alton
Location: Sioux County
Length: 2.0 miles
Surface: Crushed stone

Contact:
Mel D. Elsberry, Director
Orange City Parks & Recreation Department
City Hall
Orange City, IA 51041
(712)737-4885

㉖ Raccoon River Valley Trail

Endpoints: Waukee to Yale
Location: Dallas and Guthrie Counties
Length: 34.0 miles
Surface: Asphalt

Dallas County Section
Contact:
Jeff Logsdon, Director
Dallas County Conservation Board
1477 K Avenue
Perry, IA 50220-8101
(515)465-3577

Guthrie County Section
Contact:
Joe Hanner, Director
Guthrie County
Conservation Board
RR 2, Box 4A17
Panora, IA 50216-9802
(515)755-3061

㉗ Ringgold Trailway

Endpoints: Mount Ayr
Location: Ringgold County
Length: 2.0 miles
Surface: Original ballast

Contact:
Rick Hawkins, Director
Ringgold County
Conservation Board
P.O. Box 83A, RR 1
Mount Ayr, IA 50854
(515)464-2787

㉘ Russell White Nature Trail

Endpoints: Lanesboro
Location: Carroll County
Length: 3.8 miles
Surface: Original ballast and grass

Contact:
David Olson, Director
Carroll County
Conservation Board
RR 1, Box 240A
Carroll, IA 51401-9801
(712)792-4614

㉙ Sauk Trail

Endpoints: Carroll to Lake View
Location: Carroll and Sac Counties
Length: 13.0 miles of 33.2-mile trail is on abandoned rail corridor
Surface: Asphalt and crushed stone

Carroll County Section

Contact:
David Olson, Director
Carroll County
Conservation Board
RR 1, Box 240A
Carroll, IA 51401-9801
(712)792-4614

Sac County Section

Contact:
Chris Bass, Director
Sac County Conservation Board
2970 280th Street
Sac City, IA 50583-7474
(712)662-4530

㉚ Shell Rock River Trail

Endpoints: Clarksville to Shell Rock
Location: Butler County
Length: 5.5 miles
Surface: Crushed stone

Contact:
Steve Brunsma, Director
Butler County Conservation Board
28727 Timber Road
Clarksville, IA 50619
(319)278-4237

㉛ Shimek Forest Trail

Endpoints: Shimek State Forest
Location: Lee and Van Buren Counties
Length: 4.5 miles (will be 6.0 miles when completed)
Surface: Original ballast, grass and dirt

Contact:
Wayne Fuhlbrugge
Area Forester
Shimek State Forest
RR 1, Box 95
Farmington, IA 52626
(319)878-3811

㉜ Solon–Lake Macbride Recreation Trail

Endpoints: Solon to Lake Macbride State Park
Location: Johnson County
Length: 0.3 miles of 5.3-mile trail is on abandoned rail corridor
Surface: Gravel

Contact:
Bill Mishler, Ranger
Lake Macbride State Park
Solon, IA 52333
(319)644-2200

㉝ Three Rivers Trail

Endpoints: Eagle Grove to Rolfe
Location: Humboldt, Pocahontas and Wright Counties
Length: 36.0 miles (will be 49.0 miles when completed)
Surface: Crushed stone

Contact:
Jeanne Mae Ballgous
Director
Humboldt County
Conservation Board
Court House
Dakota City, IA 50529
(515)332-4087

㉞ Upper Nish Habitat Trail

Endpoints: Irwin
Location: Shelby County
Length: 4.0 miles
Surface: Original ballast and dirt

Contact:
Darby Sanders, Director
Shelby County
Conservation Board
514 Maple Road
Harlan, IA 51537
(712)755-2628

35 Wabash Trace Nature Trail

Endpoints: Council Bluffs to Blanchard
Location: Fremont, Mills, Page and Pottawattamie Counties
Length: 63 miles (will be 83 miles when completed)
Surface: Crushed stone

on certain sections

Contact:
Pete Philips, Vice President
Southwest Iowa Nature
Trails, Inc.
347 Hyde Avenue
Council Bluffs, IA 51503
(712)328-6836

36 Wapsi–Great Western Trail

Endpoints: Riceville
Location: Mitchell County
Length: 4 miles (will be 10.5 miles when completed)
Surface: Crushed stone

on certain sections

Contact:
Elaine Govern, Chairman
Wapsi-Great Western Line
Committee
P.O. Box 116
Riceville, IA 50466-0116
(515)985-4030

37 Winkel Memorial Trail

Endpoints: Sibley to Allendorf with spur to Willow Creek County Recreation Area
Location: Osceola County
Length: 6.0 miles of 10.0-mile trail is on abandoned rail corridor
Surface: Gravel

Contact:
Ron Spengler, Director
Osceola County
Conservation Board
5945 Highway 9
Ocheyedan, IA 51354
(712)758-3709

38 Winnebago River Trail

Endpoints: Forest City
Location: Winnebago County
Length: 2.5 miles (will be 6.0 miles when completed)
Surface: Crushed stone, original ballast and wood chips

Contact:
Robert Schwartz
Executive Director
Winnebago County
Conservation Board
33496 110th Avenue
Forest City, IA 50436-9205
(515)565-3390

39 Winneshiek County Trail

Endpoints: Calmar to Winneshiek County line
Location: Winneshiek County
Length: 17.0 miles of 18.0-mile trail is on abandoned rail corridor
Surface: Crushed stone

on certain sections

Contact:
David Oestmann, Director
Winneshiek County
Conservation Board
2546 Lake Meyer Road
Fort Atkinson, IA 52144
(319)534-7145

40 Yellow River Forest Trail

Endpoints: Yellow River State Forest
Location: Allamakee County
Length: 5.0 miles of 25.0-mile trail is on abandoned rail corridor
Surface: Gravel, grass and dirt

Contact:
Bob Honeywell
Area Forester
Yellow River State Forest
729 State Forest Road
Harpers Ferry, IA 52146
(319)586-2254

Kansas

❷ Whistle Stop Park

Endpoints: Elkhart
Location: Morton County
Length: 1.3 miles of 1.8-mile trail is on abandoned rail corridor
Surface: Asphalt with parallel grass treadway

Contact:
Ed Johnson, Chairman
Whistle Stop Park
Committee
Drawer 70
Elkhart, KS 67950
(316)647-2402

❶ Lawrence Rail-Trail

Endpoints: Lawrence
Location: Douglas County
Length: 1.0 mile
Surface: Crushed stone and original ballast

Contact:
Fred DeVictor
Director
Lawrence Parks and
Recreation Department
P.O. Box 708
Lawrence, KS 66044-0708
(913)832-3000

Kentucky

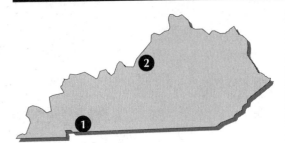

❷ River Walk Trail

Endpoints: Louisville
Location: Jefferson County
Length: 0.2 miles (will be 4.7 miles when completed)
Surface: Asphalt

Contact:
Sushil Gupta
Manager of Urban Design
& Forestry
City Hall, Room 217
601 West Jefferson
Louisville, KY 40202
(502)574-3921

❶ Cadiz Railroad Trail

Endpoints: Cadiz
Location: Trigg County
Length: 1.5 miles
Surface: Asphalt

Contact:
Stan White, Chairman
Cadiz Railroad Trail
Committee
P.O. Drawer B
Cadiz, KY 42211
(502)522-8483

LOUISIANA

❶ Tammany Trace Trail

Endpoints: Covington
Location: St. Tammany County
Length: 8.5 miles (will be 31.0 mile when completed)
Surface: Asphalt

Contact:
Felicia Leonard
Transportation Planner
St. Tammany Parish Police
Jury Dept. of Development
428 East Boston Street
P.O. Box 628
Covington, LA 70434
(504)898-2524

MAINE

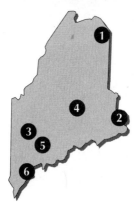

❶ Aroostook Valley Right-of-Way

Endpoints: Washburn to Van Buren
Location: Aroostook County
Length: 71.0 mile
Surface: Gravel and original ballast

Contact:
Scott Ramsey, Supervisor
Off Road Vehicles
Bureau of Parks & Recreation
Department of Conservation, #22
Augusta, ME 04333
(207)287-3821

---

❷ Calais Waterfront Walkway

Endpoints: Calais
Location: Washington County
Length: 0.3 miles (will be 1.5 miles when completed)
Surface: Gravel

Contact:
Scott Haerman
Executive Director
Greater Calais Area
Chamber of Commerce
P.O. Box 368
Calais, ME 04619
(207)454-2308

❸ Jay to Farmington Trail

Endpoints: Jay to Farmington
Location: Franklin County
Length: 14.0 miles
Surface: Gravel and original ballast

Contact:
Scott Ramsey, Supervisor
Off Road Vehicles
Bureau of Parks & Recreation
Department of Conservation, #22
Augusta, ME 04333
(207)287-3821

❹ Lagrange Right-of-Way Trail

Endpoints: South Lagrange to Medford
Location: Penobscot and Piscataquis Counties
Length: 12.0 miles
Surface: Gravel and original ballast

Contact:
Scott Ramsey, Supervisor
Off Road Vehicles
Bureau of Parks &
Recreation
Department of
Conservation, #22
Augusta, ME 04333
(207)287-3821

❺ Old Narrow Gauge Volunteer Nature Trail

Endpoints: Randolph
Location: Kennebec County
Length: 2.4 miles
Surface: Original ballast and dirt

 on certain sections

Contact:
Wayne Libby
Town of Randolph
Code Enforcement &
Public Works
P.O. Box 216
Randolph, ME 04345-0216
(207)582-0335

❻ South Portland Greenbelt

Endpoints: South Portland
Location: Cumberland County
Length: 3.5 miles (will be 4.5 miles when completed)
Surface: Asphalt

Contact:
Tex Haeuser
Planning Director
City Hall
25 Cottage Road
South Portland, ME 04106
(207)767-3201

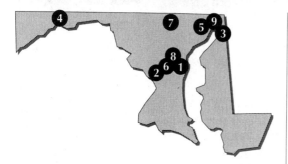

❶ Baltimore and Annapolis Trail

Endpoints: Glen Burnie to Annapolis
Location: Anne Arundel County
Length: 13.3 miles
Surface: Asphalt

Contact:
David Dionne
Park Superintendent
Baltimore and Annapolis Trail Park
P.O. Box 1007
Severna Park, MD 21146
(410)222-6244

❷ Capital Crescent Trail

Endpoints: Silver Spring to Washington, DC
Location: Montgomery County and District of Columbia
Length: 7.0 miles open in two separate sections (will be 11.0 miles when completed)
Surface: Asphalt

Montgomery County Section

Contact:
William Gries
Montgomery County
Department of Parks
9500 Brunett Avenue
Silver Spring, MD 20901
(301)495-2535

Washington, DC Section

Contact:
Rich Metzinger
Landscape Architect
National Park Service
National Capital Region
1100 Ohio Drive, SW
Washington, DC 20242
(202)523-5555

❸ Chesapeake & Delaware Canal Trail

Endpoints: Chesapeake City to Delaware City
Location: Cecil and New Castle Counties
Length: 15.0 miles
Surface: Crushed stone and dirt

Contact:
David Hawley, Civil Engineer
U.S. Army Corps of Engineers
P.O. Box 77
Chesapeake City, MD 21915
(410)885-5621

❹ Chesapeake & Ohio Canal National Historic Park

Endpoints: Cumberland to Georgetown
Location: Allegany and Washington Counties
Length: 184.5 miles
Surface: Crushed stone, gravel and dirt

 on certain sections

Contact:
Douglas Faris
Superintendent
C&O National Heritage Park
P.O. Box 4
Sharpsburg, MD 21782
(301)739-4200

❺ Lower Susquehanna Heritage Greenway

Endpoints: Susquehanna State Park to Conowingo Dam
Location: Harford County
Length: 2.5 miles of 50.0-mile trail is on abandoned rail corridor
Surface: Dirt

Contact:
Rick Smith, Manager
Rocks Susquehanna State Park
3318 Rocks Chrome Hill Road
Jarrettsville, MD 21084
(410)836-6735

❻ Mill Trail

Endpoints: Savage Park
Location: Howard County
Length: 1.0 mile (will be 5.5 miles when completed)
Surface: Gravel and original ballast

Contact:
Clara Govin
Senior Park Planner
Howard County Recreation & Parks
7120 Oakland Mills Road
Columbia, MD 21046
(410)313-4700

❼ Northern Central Railroad Trail

Endpoints: Ashland to Pennsylvania state line
Location: Baltimore County
Length: 21.0 mile
Surface: Crushed stone

Contact:
Peyton Taylor
Area Manager
Gunpowder Falls State Park
P.O. Box 5032
Glen Arm, MD 21057
(410)592-2897

❽ Number Nine Trolley Line

Endpoints: Baltimore
Location: Baltimore County
Length: 2.0 miles
Surface: Asphalt

Contact:
William Lambert
Western Region Superintendent
Baltimore County Department of Recreation & Parks
301 Washington Avenue
Towson, MD 21204
(410)887-3829

❾ Octararo Trail

Endpoints: Colora to Sylmar
Location: Cecil County
Length: 6.0 miles
Surface: Wood chips

Contact:
Edward W. Slicer
Director
Parks & Recreation
P.O. Box 725
Rising Sun, MD 21911
(410)392-4537

❶ Cape Cod Rail Trail

Endpoints: Dennis to South Wellfleet
Location: Barnstable County
Length: 25.0 miles
Surface: Asphalt with parallel dirt treadway

Contact:
Steve Nicole, Park Manager
Nickerson State Park
3488 Main Street
Brewster, MA 02631
(508)896-3491

❷ Falmouth Shining Sea Trail

Endpoints: Falmouth to Woods Hole
Location: Barnstable County
Length: 3.2 miles (will be 4.0 miles when completed)
Surface: Asphalt with parallel dirt treadway

Contact:
Kevin Lynch, Chairman
Falmouth Bikeways Committee
P.O. Box 2372
Teaticket, MA 02536
(508)968-5859

❸ Minuteman Bikeway

Endpoints: Arlington to Bedford
Location: Middlesex County
Length: 11.0 miles
Surface: Asphalt

Contact:
Alan McClennen, Jr.
Director
Planning and Community Development
Town of Arlington
730 Massachusetts Avenue
Arlington, MA 02174
(617)641-4891

❹ Northampton Bikeway

Endpoints: Northampton
Location: Hampshire County
Length: 2.6 miles
Surface: Asphalt

Contact:
Wayne Feiden
Principal Planner
Northampton Office
Planning and Development
210 Main Streeet
Northampton, MA 01060
(413)586-6950

❺ Norwottuck Rail-Trail

Endpoints: Amherst to Northampton
Location: Hampshire County
Length: 9 miles (will be 10 miles when completed)
Surface: Concrete

Contact:
Daniel O'Brien
Bikeway Planner
Dept. of Environmental Management
100 Cambridge Street
Room 1404
Boston, MA 02202
(617)727-3160

❻ Quarries Footpath

Endpoints: Quincy
Quarries Historic Site
Location: Norfolk County
Length: 1.0 mile
Surface: Dirt

Contact:
Maggie Brown
Chief Ranger
Blue Hills Reservation,
South Region
695 Hillside Street
Milton, MA 02186
(617)727-4573

❼ Southern New England Trunkline Trail

Endpoints: Franklin to
Willamantic, CT
Location: Norfolk and
Worcester Counties
Length: 55.0 miles
Surface: Gravel and original ballast

Contact:
Daniel O'Brien
Bikeway Planner
Dept. of Environmental
Management
100 Cambridge Street
Room 1404
Boston, MA 02202
(617)727-3160

❽ Southwest Corridor Park

Endpoints: Boston
Location: Suffolk County
Length: 5.0 miles
Surface: Asphalt

Contact:
Allan Morris
Parkland Manager
Southwest Corridor Park
38 New Heath Street
Jamaica Plain, MA 02130
(617)727-0057

❶ Aspen Trail

Endpoints: Grayling
Location: Crawford County
Length: 1.1 miles of 3.0-mile trail is on abandoned rail corridor
Surface: Gravel, grass and dirt

Contact:
Robert Bacon, Supervisor
Management Unit
Hartwick Pines State Park
Route 3, Box 3840
Grayling, MI 49738-9357
(517)348-7068

❷ Battle Creek Linear Park

Endpoints: Battle Creek
Location: Calhoun County
Length: 0.5 miles of 17.0-mile trail is on abandoned rail corridor
Surface: Asphalt

Contact:
Linn Kracht
Superintendent of Facilities
Battle Creek Department of Parks and Recreation
124 East Michigan Avenue
Battle Creek, MI 49017
(616)966-3431

③ Baw Beese Trail

Endpoints: Hillsdale
Location: Hillsdale
County
Length: 2.2 miles (will be
6.0 miles when completed)
Surface: Original ballast

Contact:
Mark Reynolds, Director
Hillsdale Recreation Dept.
43 McCollum Street
Hillsdale, MI 49242-1630
(517)437-3579

④ Bay Hampton Rail Trail

Endpoints: Bay City to
Hampton Township
Location: Bay County
Length: 4.0 miles of 6.0-
mile trail is on abandoned
rail corridor
Surface: Asphalt

Bay City Section
Contact:
Al McFayden
City of Bay City
301 Washington Street
Bay City, MI 48708
(517)894-8154

Hampton Section
Contact:
Peg Vansummeran
Hampton Township
P.O. Box 187
Bay City, MI 48707
(517)893-7541

⑤ Beaver Lodge Nature Trail

Endpoints: Ottawa
National Forest
Location: Houghton
County
Length: 0.3 miles of 1.3-
mile trail is on abandoned
rail corridor
Surface: Grass, wood
chips and dirt

Contact:
Dawn Buss
Forestry Technician
Ottawa National Forest
1209 Rockland Road
Ontonagon, MI 49953
(906)884-2411

⑥ Bergland to Sidnaw Rail Trail

Endpoints: Sidnaw to
Bergland
Location: Houghton and
Ontonagon Counties
Length: 45.0 miles
Surface: Gravel and dirt

   on certain
sections

Contact:
Martin Nelson
Area Forest Manager
Copper Country State Forest
P.O. Box 400
Baraga, MI 49908-0400
(906)353-6651

⑦ Big "M" Cross Country Ski Trail

Endpoints: Manistee
National Forest
Location: Manistee
County
Length: 0.8 miles of 18.6-
mile trail is on abandoned
rail corridor
Surface: Grass and dirt

Contact:
Teresa Maday
Outdoor Recreation
Planner
Manistee National Forest
1658 Manistee Highway
Manistee, MI 49660-9616
(616)723-2211

⑧ Big Bear Lake Nature Pathway

Endpoints: Mackinaw
State Forest
Location: Otsego County
Length: 0.3 miles of 2.2-
mile trail is on abandoned
rail corridor
Surface: Dirt

Contacts:
Duane Hoffman
District Fire & Recreation
Specialist
Mackinaw State Forest
P.O. Box 667
Gaylord, MI 49735-0667
(517)732-3541

William Karnes
Forest Technician
Department of Natural
Resources
P.O. Box 667
Gaylord, MI 49735
(517)732-3541

46

❾ Bill Nicholls Trail

Endpoints: Houghton to McKeever
Location: Houghton and Ontonagon Counties
Length: 40.6 miles of 55.0-mile trail is on abandoned rail corridor
Surface: Original ballast

Contact:
Martin Nelson
or Dave Tuovila
Copper Country State Forest
P.O. Box 440
Baraga, MI 49908
(906)353-6651

❿ Boardwalk of Grand Haven

Endpoints: Grand Haven
Location: Ottawa County
Length: 0.8 miles of 2.5-mile trail is on abandoned rail corridor
Surface: Asphalt and wood-planks

Contact:
Teresa Jones
or Laurel Nease
Grand Haven Visitors Bureau
One South Harbor Drive
Grand Haven, MI 49417
(616)842-4499

⓫ Bruno's Run Trail

Endpoints: Munsing
Location: Alger County
Length: 0.8 miles of 7.3-mile trail is on abandoned rail corridor
Surface: Dirt

Contact:
Richard Andersen
Recreation Supervisor
Hiawatha National Forest
Munising Ranger District
400 East Munising
Munising, MI 49862-1487
(906)387-2512

⓬ Cass City Walking Trail

Endpoints: Cass City
Location: Tuscola County
Length: 1.4 miles
Surface: Gravel and original ballast

Contact:
Lou LaPonsie
Village Manager
6737 Church Street
P.O. Box 123
Cass City, MI 48726
(517)872-2911

⓭ Chelsea Hospital Fitness Trail

Endpoints: Chelsea
Location: Washtenaw County
Length: 0.3 miles of 1.0-mile trail is on abandoned rail corridor
Surface: Wood chips

Contact:
Phillip Boham
Vice President
Chelsea Community Hospital
775 South Main Street
Chelsea, MI 48118
(313)475-3998

⓮ Coalwood Trail

Endpoints: Shingleton to Chatham
Location: Alger and Schoolcraft Counties
Length: 24.0 miles
Surface: Original ballast

Contacts:
Dick Anderson
Assistant Ranger
Hiawatha National Forest
Munising Ranger District
400 East Munising, RR #2
Box 400
Munising, MI 49862
(906)387-2512

Bruce Veneberg
Area Forest Manager
Lake Superior State Forest
Shingleton Forest Area
M-28, P.O. Box 57
Shingleton, MI 49884
(906)452-6227

⑮ Deer Run Trail

Endpoints: Hartwick Pines State Park
Location: Crawford County
Length: 1.0 mile of 5.0-mile trail is on abandoned rail corridor
Surface: Gravel, grass and dirt

Contact:
Robert Bacon, Supervisor
Management Unit
Hartwick Pines State Park
Route 3, Box 3840
Grayling, MI 49738-9357
(517)348-7068

⑯ Felch Grade Trail

Endpoints: Narenta to Felch
Location: Delta, Dickinson and Menominee Counties
Length: 40.0 miles of 45.0-mile trail is on abandoned rail corridor
Surface: Gravel and dirt

Contact:
Russ MacDonald
Asst. Area Forest Manager
Escanaba Forest Area
Escanaba River State Forest
6833 US 2
Gladstone, MI 49870
(906)786-2354

⑰ Frank N. Anderson Trail

Endpoints: Bay City State Park
Location: Bay County
Length: 1.4 miles
Surface: Asphalt

Contact:
Karen Gillispie
Bay City State Park
3582 State Park Drive
Bay City, MI 48706-1157
(517)684-3020

⑱ Freda Trail

Endpoints: Freda to Bill Nicholls Trail
Location: Houghton County
Length: 11.2 miles
Surface: Original ballast

Contact:
Martin Nelson
or Dave Tuovila
Copper Country State Forest
P.O. Box 400
Baraga, MI 49908
(906)353-6651

⑲ Gallup Trail

Endpoints: Ann Arbor
Location: Washtenaw County
Length: 3.0 miles
Surface: Asphalt

Contact:
Tom Raynes, Manager
Ann Arbor Department of Parks & Recreation
P.O. Box 8647
Ann Arbor, MI 48107
(313)994-2780

⑳ Gay Trail

Endpoints: Gay to Mohawk
Location: Houghton and Keweenaw Counties
Length: 12.0 miles of 27.0-mile trail is on abandoned rail corridor
Surface: Original ballast

Contact:
Martin Nelson
Area Forest Manager
Copper Country State Forest
P.O. Box 400
Baraga, MI 49908-0400
(906)353-6651

㉑ Grand Marais Trail

Endpoints: Shingleton to Grand Marais
Location: Alger and Schoolcraft Counties
Length: 13.0 miles of 41.7-mile trail is on abandoned rail corridor
Surface: Sand

Contact:
Bruce Veneberg
Area Forest Manager
Lake Superior State Forest
Shingleton Forest Area M-28
Shingleton, MI 49884
(906)452-6227

㉒ Grass River Natural Area Nature Trail

Endpoints: Bellaire
Location: Antrim County
Length: 4.0 miles
Surface: Crushed stone, original ballast and dirt

Contact:
Mark Randolph
Grass River Natural Area
P.O. Box 231
Bellaire, MI 49615-0231
(616)533-8314

㉓ Hancock/Calumet Trail

Endpoints: Hancock to Calumet
Location: Houghton County
Length: 13.0 miles
Surface: Gravel and dirt

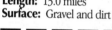

Contact:
Martin Nelson
or Dave Tuovila
Copper Country State Forest
P.O. Box 400
Baraga, MI 49908
(906)353-6651

㉔ Hart–Montague Bicycle Trail State Park

Endpoints: Hart to Montague
Location: Muskegon and Oceana Counties
Length: 22.5 miles
Surface: Asphalt

Contact:
Peter Lundborg
Park Manager
Silver Lake State Park
9679 West State Park Road
Mears, MI 49436-9734
(616)873-3083

㉕ Haywire Trail

Endpoints: Manistique to Shingleton
Location: Alger and Schoolcraft Counties
Length: 33.0 miles
Surface: Original ballast and cinder

Contacts:
Dick Anderson
Assistant Ranger
Hiawatha National Forest
Munising Ranger District
400 East Munising, RR #2
Box 400
Munising, MI 49862
(906)387-2512

Bruce Veneberg
Area Forest Manager
Lake Superior State Forest
Shingleton Forest Area
M-28, P.O. Box 57
Shingleton, MI 49884
(906)452-6227

㉖ Houghton Waterfront Trail

Endpoints: Houghton
Location: Houghton County
Length: 2.0 miles of 4.5-mile trail is on abandoned rail corridor
Surface: Asphalt

Contact:
Scott MacInnes
Assistant City Manager
City of Houghton
P.O. Box 406
Houghton, MI 49931-0406
(906)482-1700

㉗ Huron Forest Snowmobile Trails

Endpoints: Huron National Forest to Barton City
Location: Alcona and Oscoda Counties
Length: 11.0 miles of 95.0-mile trail is on abandoned rail corridor
Surface: Dirt

Contact:
Nick Schmelter
Assistant Ranger
Huron National Forest
Huron Shores Ranger District
5761 Skeel Avenue
Oscoda, MI 48750
(517)739-0728

㉘ Iron Range Trails

Endpoints: Crystal Falls to Iron River
Location: Iron County
Length: 25.0 miles
Surface: Original ballast

  on certain sections

Contact:
Dave Tuovila
District Fire & Recreation Specialist
Copper Country State Forest
P.O. Box 440
Baraga, MI 49908
(906)353-6651

㉙ Iron's Area Tourist Association Snowmobile Trail

Endpoints: Manistee National Forest
Location: Lake, Manistee and Wexford Counties
Length: 22.0 miles
Surface: Original ballast

Contact:
John Hojnowski
Assistant Ranger
Manistee Ranger District
1658 Manistee Highway
Manistee, MI 49660
(616)723-2211

㉚ Jordan River Pathway

Endpoints: Jordan River Valley
Location: Antrim County
Length: 0.5 miles of 18.0-mile trail is on abandoned rail corridor
Surface: Dirt

Contact:
Bill Karnes or Bill O'Neill
Michigan Department of Natural Resources
P.O. Box 667
Gaylord, MI 49735
(517)732-3541

㉛ Jordan Valley Snowmobile Trail

Endpoints: Jordan Valley
Location: Antrim and Charlevoix Counties
Length: 8.0 miles of 33.0-mile trail is on abandoned rail corridor
Surface: Original ballast

Contact:
Duane Hoffman
District Fire & Recreation Specialist
Mackinaw State Forest
P.O. Box 667
Gaylord, MI 49735-0667
(517)732-3541

㉜ Kal-Haven Trail Sesquicentennial State Park Trail

Endpoints: Kalamazoo to South Haven
Location: Kalamazoo and Van Buren Counties
Length: 33.5 miles
Surface: Crushed stone with parallel dirt treadway

Contact:
David Marsh
Trail Supervisor
Van Buren State Park
23960 Ruggles Road
South Haven, MI 49090
(616)637-4984

❸❸ Kent Trails

Endpoints: Grand Rapids
Location: Kent County
Length: 7.5 miles of 15.0-mile trail is on abandoned rail corridor
Surface: Asphalt

Contact:
Roger Sabine
Asst. Director of Planning
Kent County Road and Park Commission
1500 Scribner NW
Grand Rapids, MI 49504
(616)242-6948

❸❹ Keweenaw Trail

Endpoints: Houghton to Calumet
Location: Houghton and Keweenaw Counties
Length: 38.0 miles of 58.0-mile trail is on abandoned rail corridor
Surface: Grass and dirt

Contact:
Martin Nelson
or Dave Tuovila
Copper Country State Forest
P.O. Box 400
Baraga, MI 49908
(906)353-6651

❸❺ Kiwanis Trail

Endpoints: Adrian to Tecumseh
Location: Lenawee County
Length: 8.0 miles
Surface: Asphalt and original ballast

 on certain sections

Contact:
Mark Gasche, Director
Community Services
Adrian City Hall
100 E. Church Street
Adrian, MI 49221
(517)263-2161

❸❻ L'Anse to Big Bay Trail

Endpoints: L'Anse to Big Bay
Location: Baraga and Marquette Counties
Length: 7.0 miles of 54.0-mile trail is on abandoned rail corridor
Surface: Dirt

Contact:
Martin Nelson
Area Forest Manager
Copper Country State Forest
P.O. Box 400
Baraga, MI 49908-0400
(906)353-6651

❸❼ Lakelands Trail State Park

Endpoints: Pinckney to Stockbridge
Location: Ingham, Jackson, Livingston and Oakland Counties
Length: 12.5 miles (will be 36 miles when completed)
Surface: Crushed stone with parallel gravel treadway

Contact:
Jon LaBossiere
Pinckney Recreation Area
8555 Silver Hill
Pinckney, MI 48169-8901
(313)426-4913

❸❽ Lakeside Trail

Endpoints: Spring Lake
Location: Ottawa County
Length: 1.8 miles
Surface: Asphalt

Contact:
Andy Lukasik
Administrative Assistant
Village of Spring Lake
102 W. Savidge Street
Spring Lake, MI 49456
(616)842-1393

㊴ Lansing River Trail

Endpoints: Lansing
Location: Ingham County
Length: 1.0 mile of 6.0-mile trail is on abandoned rail corridor
Surface: Asphalt

Contact:
Dick Schaefer
Landscape Architect
Parks & Recreation
124 West Michigan
Lansing, MI 48933
(517)483-4277

㊵ Little Falls Trail

Endpoints: Ottawa National Forest
Location: Gogebic and Ontonagon Counties
Length: 5.5 miles of 6.5-mile trail is on abandoned rail corridor
Surface: Original ballast and grass

Contact:
Wayne Petterson
Forestry Technician
Ottawa National Forest
P.O. Box 276
Watersmeet, MI 49969-0276
(906)358-4551

㊶ Little Traverse Wheelway

Endpoints: Petoskey
Location: Emmet County
Length: 1.0 mile of 2.3-mile trail is on abandoned rail corridor
Surface: Asphalt

Contact:
Brad Leech, City Planner
City of Petoskey
100 West Lake St.
Petoskey, MI 49770-2349
(616)347-2500

㊷ Mackinaw/Alanson Trail

Endpoints: Mackinaw to Alanson
Location: Emmet County
Length: 24.0 miles
Surface: Gravel, grass and dirt

Contact:
Duane Hoffman
District Fire & Recreation Management Specialist
Mackinaw State Forest
P.O. Box 667
Gaylord, MI 49735
(517)732-3541

㊸ Mertz Grade Trail

Endpoints: Hartwick Pines State Park
Location: Crawford County
Length: 1.6 miles of 2.5-mile trail is on abandoned rail corridor
Surface: Gravel, grass and dirt

Contact:
Robert Bacon, Supervisor
Management Unit
Hartwick Pines State Park
Route 3, Box 3840
Grayling, MI 49738-9357
(517)348-7068

㊹ Michigan Shore to Shore Riding-Hiking Trail

Location: Benzie, Grand Traverse, Missaukee and Wexford Counties
Length: 75.0 miles open in two separate sections
Surface: Sand

Contact:
Steve Cross
Forest Management Specialist
Forest Management Division
8015 Mackinaw Trail
Cadillac, MI 49601-9746
(616)775-9727

Cadillac Spur Section

Endpoints: Cadillac
Length: 12.5 miles of 35.0-mile trail is on abandoned rail corridor

Scheck's Place Section

Endpoints: Empire to Sheck's Place
Length: 14.0 miles of 40.0-mile trail is on abandoned rail corridor

⑤ Nahma Grade Trail

Endpoints: Rapid River to Alger County line
Location: Delta County
Length: 16.0 miles of 32.0-mile trail is on abandoned rail corridor
Surface: Dirt

 on certain sections

Contact:
Anne Okonek
Assistant District Ranger
Hiawatha National Forest
Rapid River Ranger District
8181 U.S. Highway 2
Rapid River, MI 49878-9501
(906)474-6442

⑥ Nordhouse Dunes Trail System

Endpoints: Manistee National Forest
Location: Mason County
Length: 4.0 miles of 15.0-mile trail is on abandoned rail corridor
Surface: Grass and dirt

Contact:
Teresa Maday
Outdoor Recreation Planner
Manistee National Forest
1658 Manistee Highway
Manistee, MI 49660-9616
(616)723-2211

⑦ North Country National Scenic Trail

Location: Lake, Manistee, Mason and Newaygo Counties
Length: 44.8 miles open in three separate sections
Surface: Dirt

Baldwin Section

Endpoints: Baldwin
Length: 1.5 miles

Contact:
Patricia Allen
Executive Director
North Country Trail Association
3777 Sparks Drive, SE
Grand Rapids, MI 49546
(616)975-0831

Manistee Section

Endpoints: Red Bridge to Marilla Trailhead
Length: 0.3 miles of 43.0-mile trail is on abandoned rail corridor

Contact:
John Hojnowski or Romona Venegas
Manistee Ranger District
USDA Forest Service
1658 Manistee Highway
Manistee, MI 49660
(616)723-2211

White Cloud Section

Endpoints: White Cloud
Length: 0.3 miles

Contact:
Patricia Allen
Executive Director
North Country Trail Association
3777 Sparks Drive, SE
Grand Rapids, MI 49546
(616)975-0831

⑧ Old Grade Nature Trail

Endpoints: Glen Lake
Location: Leelanau County
Length: 1.0 mile
Surface: Grass

Contact:
William Herd
Park Ranger
Sleeping Bear Dunes National Lakeshore
9922 Front Street
Empire, MI 49630-0277
(616)326-5134

⑭ Old Grade Trail

Endpoints: North Manitou Island
Location: Leelanau County
Length: 1.7 miles of 8.0-mile trail is on abandoned rail corridor
Surface: Grass and dirt

Contact:
William Herd, Park Ranger
Sleeping Bear Dunes
National Lakeshore
9922 Front Street
Empire, MI 49630-0277
(616)326-5134

⑮ Paint Creek Trailway

Endpoints: Lake Orion to Rochester Hills
Location: Oakland County
Length: 10.0 miles of 10.5-mile trail is on abandoned rail corridor
Surface: Crushed stone, original ballast and dirt

Contact:
Linda Gorecki
Trailways Coordinator
Paint Creek Trailways
Commission
4393 Collins Road
Rochester, MI 48306-1619
(810)651-9260

⑯ Pere Marquette Rail-Trail of Mid-Michigan

Endpoints: Midland to Clare
Location: Midland County
Length: 22 miles (will be 31.5 miles when completed)
Surface: Asphalt

Contact:
William C. Gibson, Director
Midland County Parks and
Recreation Department
220 West Ellsworth Street
Midland, MI 48640-5194
(517)832-6876

⑰ Pere-Marquette State Trail

Endpoints: Baldwin to Clare
Location: Clare, Lake and Osceola Counties
Length: 54.0 miles
Surface: Original ballast

Contact:
Philip Wells
Trailways Program Leader
Michigan Department of
Natural Resources
Forest Management
Division
P.O. Box 30452
Lansing, MI 48909
(517)335-3038

⑱ Peshekee to Clowry ORV Trail

Endpoints: Champion
Location: Marquette County
Length: 6.1 miles
Surface: Gravel, original ballast and dirt

Contact:
Dennis Nezich
Area Forest Manager
Ishpeming Forest Area
Escanaba River State Forest
1985 US-41
Ishpeming, MI 49849
(906)485-1031

⑲ Platte Plains Trail

Endpoints: Sleepy Bear Dunes National Lake Shore
Location: Benzie County
Length: 0.8 miles of 14.7-mile trail is on abandoned rail corridor
Surface: Grass, dirt and sand

Contact:
William Herd, Park Ranger
Sleeping Bear Dunes
National Lakeshore
9922 Front Street
Empire, MI 49630-0277
(616)326-5134

55 Railroad Trail

Endpoints: Frederick to Gaylord
Location: Crawford County
Length: 22.0 miles
Surface: Dirt

Contact:
Phil Silverio-Mazzela
Director
Alpine Snowmobile Trails, Inc.
2583 Old 27
Gaylord, MI 49735
(517)732-7171

56 Republic– Champion Grade Trail

Endpoints: Champion to Republic
Location: Marquette County
Length: 8.1 miles
Surface: Original ballast

Contact:
Dennis Nezich
Area Forest Manager
Ishpeming Forest Area
Escanaba River State Forest
1985 US-41
Ishpeming, MI 49849
(906)485-1031

57 Rivertrail Park

Endpoints: Portland
Location: Ionia County
Length: 2.6 miles of 3.7-mile trail is on abandoned rail corridor
Surface: Asphalt

Contact:
Mary Scheurer
City of Portland Parks and Recreation Department
259 Kent Street
Portland, MI 48875-1458
(517)647-7985

58 Rockland to Mass Trail

Endpoints: Rockland
Location: Ontonagon County
Length: 3.0 miles of 7.0-mile trail is on abandoned rail corridor
Surface: Original ballast

Contact:
Martin Nelson
Area Forest Manager
Copper Country State Forest
P.O. Box 400
Baraga, MI 49908-0400
(906)353-6651

59 Shingle Mill Pathway

Endpoints: Pigeon River Country Forest Area
Location: Otsego County
Length: 0.3 miles of 11.0-mile trail is on abandoned rail corridor
Surface: Dirt

Contact:
Joe Jarecki
Area Forest Manager
Pigeon River Country Forest Area
9966 Twin Lakes Road
Vanderbilt, MI 49795-9767
(517)983-4101

60 Skegemog Lake Pathway

Endpoints: Skegemog Lake Wildlife Area
Location: Kalkaska County
Length: 0.5 miles of 0.8-mile trail is on abandoned rail corridor
Surface: Original ballast

Contact:
Dennis Vitton
Area Forest Manager
Kalkaska Forest Area
2089 North Birch
Kalkaska, MI 49646
(616)258-2711

⑥ Soo/Strongs Trail

Endpoints: Sault Ste. Marie to Strongs
Location: Chippewa County
Length: 32.0 miles open in two separate sections
Surface: Original ballast and dirt

Raco to Strongs Section

Endpoints: Raco to Strongs
Length: 12.0 miles

Contact:
William Rhoe
District Ranger
Hiawatha National Forest
Sault Ste. Marie Ranger District
4000 I-75, Business Spur
Sault Ste. Marie, MI 49783
(906)635-5511

Sault Ste. Marie to Raco Section

Endpoints: Sault Ste. Marie to Raco
Length: 16.7 miles of 20.0-mile trail is on abandoned rail corridor

Contact:
Mike Renner, Area Manager
Sault Ste. Marie Forest Area
Lake Superior State Forest
P.O. Box 798
Sault Ste. Marie, MI 49783
(906)635-5281

⑥ South Lyon Rail-Trail

Endpoints: South Lyon
Location: Oakland County
Length: 2.0 miles of 2.7-mile trail is on abandoned rail corridor
Surface: Asphalt

Contact:
Rodney Cook, City Manager
City of South Lyon
214 W. Lake Street
South Lyon, MI 48178-1377
(810)437-1735

⑥ Spring Brook Pathway

Endpoints: Mackinaw State Forest
Location: Charlevoix County
Length: 0.8 miles of 6.3-mile trail is on abandoned rail corridor
Surface: Original ballast and dirt

Contact:
Bill O'Neill
Area Forest Manager
Gaylord Field Office
P.O. Box 667
Gaylord, MI 49735
(517)732-3541

⑥ St. Ignace to Trout Lake Trail

Endpoints: St. Ignace to Trout Lake
Location: Mackinac County
Length: 26.0 miles
Surface: Crushed stone

Contact:
Joe Hart
Assistant District Manager
Hiawatha National Forest
1498 West US-2
St. Ignace, MI 49781
(906)643-7900

⑥ State Line Trail

Endpoints: Wakefield to Stager
Location: Gogebic and Iron Counties
Length: 102.1 miles of 107.1-mile trail is on abandoned rail corridor
Surface: Original ballast

Contacts:
Joey Spano
West Bloomfield Parks and Recreation Commission
3325 Middlebelt Road
West Bloomfield, MI 48323-1940
(313)334-5660

Dave Tuovila
District Fire & Recreation Specialist
Copper Country State Forest
P.O. Box 440
Baraga, MI 49908
(906)353-6651

66 Tahquamenon Falls State Park Trails

Endpoints: Tahquamenon Falls State Park
Location: Chippewa and Luce Counties
Length: 35.9 miles open in three separate sections

Contact:
Jon Spieles, Park Interpreter
Tahquamenon Falls State Park
Route 48, Box 225
Paradise, MI 49768
(906)492-3415

Clark Lake Loop

Length: 3.0 miles of 5.6-mile trail is on abandoned rail corridor
Surface: Grass and dirt

North Country Loop

Length: 3.0 miles of 24.0-mile trail is on abandoned rail corridor
Surface: Grass and dirt

Wilderness Loop

Length: 3.0 miles of 6.3-mile trail is on abandoned rail corridor
Surface: Grass and dirt

67 Traverse Area Recreation Trail (TART)

Endpoints: Traverse City to Acme
Location: Grand Traverse County
Length: 2.8 miles (will be 7.8 miles when completed)
Surface: Asphalt

Contact:
Mike Dillenbeck, Manager
Grand Traverse County
Road Commission
3949 Silver Lake Road
Traverse City, MI 49684
(616)922-4848

68 Tyoga Historical Pathway

Endpoints: Deerton
Location: Alger County
Length: 0.5 miles of 1.4-mile trail is on abandoned rail corridor
Surface: Original ballast

Contact:
Dennis Nezich
Area Forest Manager
Ishpeming Forest Area
Escanaba River State Forest
1985 US-41
Ishpeming, MI 49849
(906)485-1031

69 Watersmeet/Land O'Lakes Trail

Endpoints: Watersmeet to Land O'Lakes
Location: Gogebic County
Length: 8.8 miles
Surface: Original ballast

Contact:
Wayne Petterson
Forestry Technician
Ottawa National Forest
P.O. Box 276
Watersmeet, MI 49969-0276
(906)358-4551

70 Wellston Area Tourist Association Snowmobile Trail

Endpoints: Manistee National Forest
Location: Lake and Manistee Counties
Length: 6.0 miles of 51.5-mile trail is on abandoned rail corridor
Surface: Original ballast

Contact:
Greg Peterson, Forester
Manistee Ranger District
1658 Manistee Highway
Manistee, MI 49660
(616)723-2211

ⓐ West Bloomfield Trail Network

Endpoints: West Bloomfield Township
Location: Oakland County
Length: 4.3 miles of 5.3-mile trail is on abandoned rail corridor
Surface: Crushed stone

Contact:
Sally Slater-Pierce
or Joey Spano
West Bloomfield Parks and Recreation Commission
4640 Walnut Lake Road
West Bloomfield, MI 48323
(810)334-5660

ⓑ West Campus Bicycle Path

Endpoints: Eastern Michigan University
Location: Washtenaw County
Length: 1.0 mile
Surface: Asphalt

Contact:
Dan Klenczar
Eastern Michigan University
Physical Plant
Ypsilanti, MI 48197
(313)487-4194

ⓒ White Pine Trail State Park

Endpoints: White Pine State Park
Location: Kent, Mecosta, Montcalm, Osceola and Wexford Counties
Length: 92.0 miles
Surface: Original ballast

Contact:
Paul Yauk
Michigan Department of Natural Resources
Parks and Recreation Division
P.O. Box 30257
Lansing, MI 48909
(517)335-4824

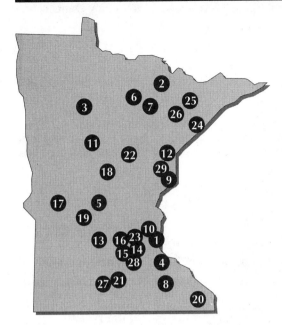

❸ Blue Ox Trail

Endpoints: Bemidji to International Falls
Location: Beltrami, Itasca and Koochiching Counties
Length: 107.3 miles
Surface: Original ballast

Contact:
Ardon Belcher
Minnesota DNR
Trails and Waterways Unit
2115 Birchmont
Beach Road, NE
Bemidji, MN 56601
(612)296-6048

❹ Cannon Valley Trail

Endpoints: Cannon Falls to Red Wing
Location: Goodhue County
Length: 19.4 miles of 19.7-mile trail is on abandoned rail corridor
Surface: Asphalt

Contact:
Bruce Blair
Superintendent
Cannon Valley Trail
City Hall
306 West Mill Street
Cannon Falls, MN 55009
(507)263-3954

❶ Afton to Lakeland Trail

Endpoints: Afton to Lakeland
Location: Washington County
Length: 2.2 miles of 3.4-mile trail is on abandoned rail corridor
Surface: Asphalt

Contact:
Jerry Skelton
P.O. Box 2050
St. Paul, MN 55109
(612)770-2311

❷ Arrowhead State Trail

Endpoints: Kabetogama State Forest
Location: Koochiching and St. Louis Counties
Length: 30.0 miles of 143.0-mile trail is on abandoned rail corridor
Surface: Original ballast

Contact:
Ron Potter
Area Supervisor
Minnesota DNR
Trails and Waterways Unit
P.O. Box 388
406 Main Street
Tower, MN 55790
(218)753-6256

❺ Central Lakes Trail

Endpoints: Avon to Fergus Falls
Location: Douglas, Grant, Otter Tail, Stearns and Todd Counties
Length: 36 miles (will be 98 miles when completed)
Surface: Gravel

Contact:
William Anderson
Trail Manager
Douglas Area Trails Association
P.O. Box 112
Alexandria, MN 56308
(612)834-2033

❻ Circle L Trail

Endpoints: Big Fork to George Washington State Forest
Location: Itasca County
Length: 2.0 miles of 24.8-mile trail is on abandoned rail corridor
Surface: Dirt

Contact:
Ben Anderson
Program Forester
Minnesota Department of Natural Resources
P.O. Box 95
Effie, MN 56639
(218)743-3694

❼ Circle T Trail

Endpoints: Nashwauk to George Washington State Forest
Location: Itasca County
Length: 3.0 miles of 39.5-mile trail is on abandoned rail corridor
Surface: Grass and dirt

Contact:
DNR Forestry
1208 E. Howard Street
Hibbing, MN 55746
(218)262-6760

❽ Douglas State Trail

Endpoints: Rochester to Pine Island
Location: Goodhue and Olmsted Counties
Length: 12.5 miles
Surface: Asphalt with parallel grass treadway

Contact:
Joel Wagar, Area Manager
Minnesota DNR
Trails and Waterways Unit
2300 Silver Creek Road, NE
Rochester, MN 55906
(507)285-7176

❾ Gandy Dancer Trail

Endpoints: St. Croix State Forest to Nemadji State Forest
Location: Carlton and Pine Counties
Length: 31.0 mile
Surface: Original ballast

Contact:
Kevin Arends
Area Supervisor
Minnesota DNR
Trails and Waterways Unit
Route 2, 701 S. Kenwood
Moose Lake, MN 55767
(218)485-5410

❿ Gateway Segment of the Willard Munger Trail

Endpoints: St. Paul to Pine Point Regional Park
Location: Ramsey and Washington Counties
Length: 19 miles (will be 20 miles when completed)
Surface: Asphalt with parallel gravel treadway

Contact:
Larry Killien
Area Supervisor
Minnesota DNR
Trails and Waterways Unit
1200 Warner Road
St. Paul, MN 55106-6793
(612)772-7935

⓫ Heartland State Trail

Endpoints: Park Rapids to Cass Lake
Location: Cass and Hubbard Counties
Length: 47.0 miles of 51.0-mile trail is on abandoned rail corridor
Surface: Asphalt and gravel with parallel grass treadway

Contact:
Pat Tangeman
Trails & Waterways Technician
Heartland State Trail
P.O. Box 112
Nevis, MN 56467-0112
(218)652-4054

⓬ Lakewalk Trail

Endpoints: Canal Park Museum to Leif Erikson Park
Location: St. Louis County
Length: 3.0 miles of 3.2-mile trail is on abandoned rail corridor
Surface: Asphalt and wood planks

Contact:
Sue Moyer, Director
Duluth Parks & Recreation Department
City Hall, Room 330
411 W. First Street
Duluth, MN 55802-1102
(218)723-3337

⓭ Luce Line Trail

Endpoints: Plymouth to Cosmos
Location: Carver, Hennepin, McLeod and Meeker Counties
Length: 65.0 miles
Surface: Crushed stone with parallel dirt treadway

 on certain sections

Contact:
Richard Schmidt
Trails & Waterways Technician
Minnesota DNR
Trails and Waterways Unit
3980 Watertown Road
Maple Plain, MN 55359-9615
(612)475-0371

⓮ Minnehaha Trail

Endpoints: Fort Snelling State Park to Minneapolis
Location: Hennepin County
Length: 2.0 miles of 5.0-mile trail is on abandoned rail corridor
Surface: Asphalt

Contact:
Bob Piotrowski
Assistant Park Manager
Fort Snelling State Park
Highway 5 and Post Road
St. Paul, MN 55111
(612)725-2390

⓯ Minnesota Valley State Trail

Endpoints: Minneapolis to Le Sueur
Location: Dakota, Hennepin and Scott Counties
Length: 4.0 miles of 75.0-mile trail is on abandoned rail corridor
Surface: Asphalt, crushed stone and dirt

 on certain sections

Contact:
Frank Knoke, Park Manager
Minnesota Valley State Recreation Area
19825 Park Boulevard
Jordan, MN 55352
(612)492-6400

⓰ Minnetonka Loop

Endpoints: Minnetonka
Location: Carver and Hennepin Counties
Length: 8.1 miles of 24.0-mile trail is on abandoned rail corridor
Surface: Crushed stone

Contact:
Robert Hill
Loop Trail Coordinator
City of Minnetonka
14600 Minnetonka Boulevard
Minnetonka, MN 55345
(612)938-7245

⑰ Minnewaska Snowmobile Trail

Endpoints: Starbuck to Villard
Location: Pope County
Length: 8.9 miles of 25.0-mile trail is on abandoned rail corridor
Surface: Gravel and dirt

Contact:
William Anderson
Trail Manager
Douglas Area Trails Association
P.O. Box 112
Alexandria, MN 56332
(612)834-2033

⑱ Paul Bunyan Trail

Endpoints: Brainerd to Hackensack
Location: Cass and Crow Wing Counties
Length: 54 miles (will be 100 miles when completed)
Surface: Asphalt

Contact:
Terry McGaughey
Paul Bunyan Trail
Volunteer Coordinator
Brainerd Area Chamber of Commerce
124 North 6th Street
Brainerd, MN 56401
(800)450-2838

⑲ Richmond to Willmar

Endpoints: Richmond to Willmar
Location: Kandiyohi and Stearns Counties
Length: 22 miles (will be 36 miles when completed)
Surface: Asphalt and crushed stone with parallel grass treadway

Contacts:
Jeff Brown, Trail Manager
Minnesota DNR
P.O. Box 508
New London, MN 56273
(612)354-4940

Gregg Soupir
Minnesota DNR
Trails and Waterways Unit
P.O. Box 457
Spicer, MN 56288-0457
(612)796-6281

⑳ Root River State Trail

Endpoints: Fountain to Rushford
Location: Fillmore and Houston Counties
Length: 37.4 miles
Surface: Asphalt and grass

Contact:
Craig Bloomer
Area Supervisor
Minnesota DNR
Trails and Waterways Unit
2300 Silver Creek Road, NE
Rochester, MN 55906
(507)285-7176

㉑ Sakatah Singing Hills State Trail

Endpoints: Faribault to Mankato
Location: Blue Earth, Le Sueur and Rice Counties
Length: 37.0 miles of 38.6-mile trail is on abandoned rail corridor
Surface: Asphalt with parallel grass treadway

Contact:
Randy Schoeneck
Trail Technician
Sakatah State Park
P.O. Box 11
Elysian, MN 56028-0011
(507)267-4772

㉒ Soo Line Trail

Endpoints: Cass Lake to Moose Lake State Park
Location: Aitkin, Carlton and Cass Counties
Length: 114.0 miles
Surface: Gravel and original ballast

Aitkin County Section
Contact:
Roger Howard
Commissioner
Aitkin County Lands Dept.
Courthouse
Aitkin, MN 56431
(218)927-2102

Carlton County Section
Contact:
Milo Rasmussen
Land Commissioner
Carlton County Lands Department
P.O. Box 130
Carlton, MN 55718-0130
(218)384-4281

Cass County Section
Contact:
Dan Marcum
Field Supervisor
Cass County Lands Department
P.O. Box 25
Pine Mountain Building
Backus, MN 56435-0025
(218)947-3338

Chippewa National Forest Section
Contact:
Bill Stocker, District Ranger
Chippewa National Forest
Route 3, Box 219
Cass Lake, MN 56633-8924
(218)335-2283

㉓ Stone Arch Bridge

Endpoints: Minneapolis
Location: Hennepin County
Length: 0.5 miles
Surface: Asphalt

Contact:
David Wiggins
Minnesota Historical Society
125 Main Street, SE
Minneapolis, MN 55414
(612)627-5433

㉔ Superior Hiking Trail

Endpoints: Split Rock Lighthouse State Park
Location: Cook, Lake and St. Louis Counties
Length: 3.0 miles of 200.0-mile trail is on abandoned rail corridor
Surface: Original ballast

Contact:
Tricia Ryan
Executive Director
Superior Hiking Trail Association
P.O. Box 4
Two Harbors, MN 55616
(218)834-4436

㉕ Taconite State Trail

Endpoints: Ely to Grand Rapids
Location: St. Louis County
Length: 21.0 mile of 176.0-mile trail is on abandoned rail corridor
Surface: Original ballast

Contact:
Ron Potter, Area Supervisor
Minnesota DNR
Trails and Waterways Unit
P.O. Box 388
406 Main Street
Tower, MN 55790
(218)753-6256

㉖ Virginia Trails

Endpoints: Virginia
Location: St. Louis County
Length: 0.3 miles of 1.0-mile trail is on abandoned rail corridor
Surface: Crushed stone and gravel

Contact:
John Bachman, Director
City of Virginia Park Department
Virginia, MN 55792
(218)741-4366

㉗ West Mankato Trail

Endpoints: Mankato City
Location: Blue Earth County
Length: 1.5 miles
Surface: Asphalt

Contact:
Floyd Roberts
Parks Superintendent
City of Mankato Parks and Forestry
P.O. Box 3368
Mankato, MN 56002-3368
(507)387-8650

㉘ West River Parkway

Endpoints: Minneapolis
Location: Hennepin County
Length: 2.0 miles (will be 5.5 miles when completed)
Surface: Asphalt and concrete

Contact:
Bob Mattson
Park & Recreation Planner
Minneapolis Park and Recreation Board
200 Grain Exchange
400 S. Fourth Street
Minneapolis, MN 55415
(612)661-4824

㉙ Willard Munger State Trail

Endpoints: Hinckley to Barnum
Location: Carlton, Pine and St. Louis Counties
Length: 55.5 miles (will be 72.5 miles when completed)
Surface: Asphalt with parallel grass treadway

Contact:
Kevin Arends
Minnesota DNR
Trails and Waterways Unit
Route 2, 701 S. Kenwood
Moose Lake, MN 55767
(218)485-5410

MISSISSIPPI

❶ Catherine "Kitty" Bryan Dill Memorial Bikeway

Endpoints: West Point
Location: Clay County
Length: 1.2 miles
Surface: Concrete

Contact:
Dewel Brasher, Jr.
City Manager
City of West Point
P.O. Box 1117
West Point, MS 39773-1117
(601)494-2573

❷ Tuxachanie National Recreation Trail

Endpoints: DeSoto National Forest
Location: Harrison and Stone Counties
Length: 10.0 miles of 22.8-mile trail is on abandoned rail corridor
Surface: Dirt

Contact:
Ed Bratcher, Forester
Biloxi Ranger District
P.O. Box 62
251 Highway 49 South
McHenry, MS 39561
(601)928-5291

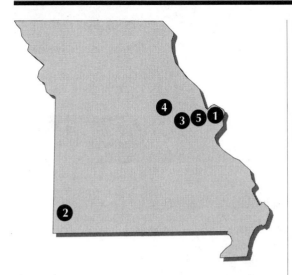

❹ M.K.T. Nature/Fitness Trail

Endpoints: Columbia
Location: Boone County
Length: 4.7 miles
Surface: Crushed stone

Contact:
Mike Hood
Superintendent of
Park Planning
City of Columbia Parks &
Recreation Department
P.O. Box N
Columbia, MO 65205
(314)874-7204

❶ Carondelet Greenway Trail

Endpoints: St. Louis
Location: St. Louis County
Length: 6.2 miles
Surface: Asphalt, crushed
stone and original ballast

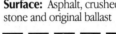

Contact:
Ted Curtis
Executive Director
Gateway Trailnet
7185 Manchester Road
St. Louis, MO 63143
(314)644-0315

❷ Frisco Greenway

Endpoints: Joplin to Webb
City
Location: Jasper County
Length: 4.0 miles
Surface: Crushed stone
and original ballast

Contact:
Paul Teverow, President
Joplin Trails Coalition
P.O. Box 2102
Joplin, MO 64803
(417)625-3114

❸ Katy Trail State Park

Endpoints: Jefferson City
to Sedalia
Location: Boone, Callaway,
Cooper, Henry, Howard,
Montgomery, St. Charles
and Warren Counties
Length: 122 miles (will be
200 miles when completed)
Surface: Crushed stone

Contact:
Kristin Allen
Katy Trail State Park
Missouri Department of
Natural Resources
P.O. Box 176
Jefferson City, MO 65102
(314)526-3809

❺ West Alton Trail

Endpoints: West Alton
Location: St. Charles
County
Length: 1.3 miles
Surface: Crushed stone

Contact:
Bill Kranz
Gateway Trailnet, Inc.
7185 Manchester Road
St. Louis, MO 63143-2441
(314)644-0315

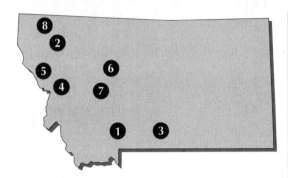

❶ Gallagator Linear Trail

Endpoints: Bozeman
Location: Gallatin County
Length: 1.5 miles
Surface: Gravel and original ballast

Contact:
Sue Harkin
Bozeman Recreation Dept.
P.O. Box 640
Bozeman, MT 59771-0640
(406)587-4724

❷ Great Northern Historical Trail

Endpoints: Kalispell to Marion
Location: Flathead County
Length: 1.2 miles (will be 23 miles when completed)
Surface: Gravel

Contact:
John Hale, President
Rails-to-Trails of Northwest Montana
P.O. Box 1103
Kalispell, MT 59903
(406)752-8383

❸ Heights Bike Trail

Endpoints: Billings
Location: Yellowstone County
Length: 2.0 miles (will be 3.5 miles when completed)
Surface: Gravel and dirt

Contact:
Mike Hink, Director
Department of Parks, Recreation and Public Lands
510 North Broadway
4th Floor Library
Billings, MT 59101-1156
(406)657-8369

❹ Kim Williams Nature Area

Endpoints: Missoula
Location: Missoula County
Length: 2.5 miles
Surface: Original ballast

Contact:
Jim Van Fossen, Director
Missoula Parks & Recreation Department
100 Hickory Street
Missoula, MT 59801
(406)721-7275

❺ NorPac Trail

Endpoints: Lolo National Forest to Idaho state line
Location: Mineral County
Length: 12.1 miles
Surface: Original ballast

Contact:
Carol Johnson
U.S. Forest Service
P.O. Box 460
109 West Riverside
Superior, MT 59872
(406)822-4233

❻ River's Edge Trail

Endpoints: Great Falls
Location: Cascade County
Length: 4.2 miles of 8.3-mile trail is on abandoned rail corridor
Surface: Asphalt and gravel

Contact:
Doug Wicks, Vice President
Friends of River's Edge Trail
P.O. Box 553
Great Falls, MT 59403
(406)761-4966

❼ Spring Meadows Lake and Centennial Park Trail

Endpoints: Helena
Location: Lewis and Clark County
Length: 1.5 miles (will be 2.3 miles when completed)
Surface: Crushed stone

Contact:
Willa Hall, President
Gold Country Rails-to-Trails
P.O. Box 434
Helena, MT 59624
(406)442-7495

❽ Tobacco River Memorial Trail

Endpoints: Kootenai National Forest
Location: Lincoln County
Length: 2.5 miles of 6.0-mile trail is on abandoned rail corridor
Surface: Gravel

Contact:
Eric Heyn
Resource Forester
Kootenai National Forest
1299 Highway 93 North
Eureka, MT 59917
(406)296-2536

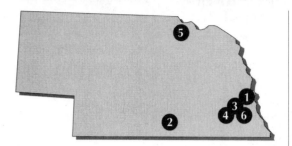

Contact:
Robert Wright
Assistant Superintendent
Lincoln Department of
Parks & Recreation
2740 A Street
Lincoln, NE 68502-3113
(402)471-7847

❶ Field Club Trail

Endpoints: Omaha
Location: Douglas County
Length: 1.5 miles
Surface: Original ballast

Contact:
Don Van Driest, President
Nebraska Trails Council
4912 South 86th Street
Omaha, NE 68127-2611
(402)339-1144

❷ Fort Kearny Hike-Bike Trail

Endpoints: Basswood
Strip State Wildlife Area to
Fort Kearny State
Recreation Area
Location: Buffalo and
Kearney Counties
Length: 1.8 miles
Surface: Original ballast

Contact:
Eugene Hunt
Superintendent
Fort Kearny State
Recreation Area
Route 4
Kearny, NE 68847
(308)865-5305

❸ MoPac East Trail

Endpoints: Lincoln to
Wabash
Location: Cass and
Lancaster Counties
Length: 18 miles (will be
26 miles when completed)
Surface: Crushed stone

Contact:
Glenn Johnson
General Manager
Lower Platte South
Natural Resource District
3125 Portia Street
P.O. Box 83581
Lincoln, NE 68501
(402)476-2729

❹ MoPac Trail

Endpoints: Lincoln
Location: Cass and
Lancaster Counties
Length: 15 miles (will be
29.2 miles when completed)
Surface: Concrete

❺ Niobrara Trail

Endpoints: Niobrara State
Park
Location: Knox County
Length: 2.1 miles
Surface: Crushed stone

Contact:
Steve Kemper
Superintendent
Niobrara State Park
P.O. Box 226
Niobrara, NE 68760
(402)857-3373

❻ Rock Island Trail

Endpoints: Lincoln
Location: Lancaster
County
Length: 5.0 miles (will be
7.0 miles when completed)
Surface: Concrete

Contact:
Robert Wright
Assistant Superintendent
Lincoln Department of
Parks & Recreation
2740 A Street
Lincoln, NE 68502-3113
(402)471-7847

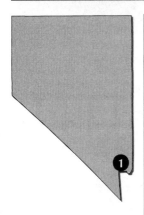

❶ Historic Railroad Hiking Trail

Endpoints: Lake Mead National Recreation Area
Location: Clark County
Length: 6.0 miles (will be 7.5 miles when completed)
Surface: Gravel and dirt

Contact:
Karen Whitney
Public Affairs Officer
Lake Mead National Recreation Area
601 Nevada Highway
Boulder City, NV 89005
(702)293-8907

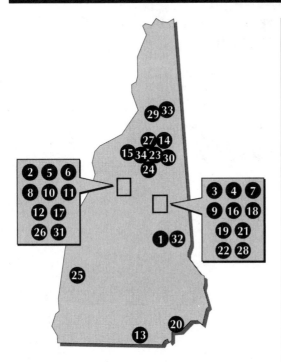

❸ Dry River Trail

Endpoints: White Mountain National Forest
Location: Carroll County
Length: 1.5 miles of 10.5-mile trail is on abandoned rail corridor
Surface: Original ballast

Contact:
Eric Swett
Forest Technician
White Mountain National Forest
Saco Ranger District
33 Kancamagus Highway
Conway, NH 03818
(603)447-5448

❹ East Branch Trail

Endpoints: White Mountain National Forest
Location: Carroll County
Length: 3.0 miles of 8.0-mile trail is on abandoned rail corridor
Surface: Original ballast

Contact:
Eric Swett
Forest Technician
White Mountain National Forest
Saco Ranger District
33 Kancamagus Highway
Conway, NH 03818
(603)447-5448

❶ Bridge-Falls Path

Endpoints: Wolfeboro
Location: Carroll County
Length: 1.0 mile
Surface: Crushed stone

Contact:
Sue Glenn
Director of Parks and Recreation
Town of Wolfeboro
P.O. Box 629
Wolfeboro, NH 03894
(603)569-5639

❷ Cedar Brook Trail

Endpoints: White Mountain National Forest
Location: Grafton County
Length: 1.5 miles of 5.7-mile trail is on abandoned rail corridor
Surface: Original ballast

Contact:
Dave Hrdlicka
Forest Technician
Pemigewassett Ranger District
White Mountain National Forest
RFD 3, Box 15
Plymouth, NH 03264
(603)536-1310

❺ East Pond Trail

Endpoints: White Mountain National Forest
Location: Grafton County
Length: 0.9 miles of 5.0-mile trail is on abandoned rail corridor
Surface: Gravel

Contact:
Dave Hrdlicka
Forest Technician
White Mountain National Forest
Pemigewassett Ranger District
RFD 3, Box 15
Plymouth, NH 03264
(603)536-1310

❻ Ethan Pond Trail

Endpoints: White Mountain National Forest
Location: Grafton County
Length: 1.5 miles of 5.6-mile trail is on abandoned rail corridor
Surface: Original ballast

Contact:
Dave Hrdlicka
Forest Technician
White Mountain National Forest
Pemigewassett Ranger District
RFD 3, Box 15
Plymouth, NH 03264
(603)536-1310

❼ Flat Mountain Pond Trail

Endpoints: White Mountain National Forest
Location: Carroll County
Length: 4.0 miles of 9.0-mile trail is on abandoned rail corridor
Surface: Original ballast

Contact:
Eric Swett
Forest Technician
White Mountain National Forest
Saco Ranger District
33 Kancamagus Highway
Conway, NH 03818
(603)447-5448

❽ Franconia Brook Trail

Endpoints: White Mountain National Forest
Location: Grafton County
Length: 5.0 miles of 7.2-mile trail is on abandoned rail corridor
Surface: Original ballast

Contact:
Dave Hrdlicka
Forest Technician
White Mountain National Forest
Pemigewassett Ranger District
RFD 3, Box 15
Plymouth, NH 03264
(603)536-1310

❾ Guinea Pond Trail

Endpoints: White Mountain National Forest
Location: Carroll County
Length: 4.0 miles
Surface: Original ballast

Contact:
Dave Hrdlicka
Forest Technician
White Mountain National Forest
Pemigewassett Ranger District
RFD 3, Box 15
Plymouth, NH 03264
(603)536-1310

❿ Lincoln Brook Trail

Endpoints: White Mountain National Forest
Location: Grafton County
Length: 0.5 miles of 6.7-mile trail is on abandoned rail corridor
Surface: Original ballast

Contact:
Dave Hrdlicka
Forest Technician
White Mountain National Forest
Pemigewassett Ranger District
RFD 3, Box 15
Plymouth, NH 03264
(603)536-1310

71

⑪ Lincoln Woods Trail

Endpoints: White Mountain National Forest
Location: Grafton County
Length: 2.7 miles
Surface: Original ballast

Contact:
Dave Hrdlicka
Forest Technician
White Mountain National Forest
Pemigewassett Ranger District
RFD 3, Box 15
Plymouth, NH 03264
(603)536-1310

⑫ Little East Pond Trail

Endpoints: White Mountain National Forest
Location: Grafton County
Length: 0.8 miles of 1.7-mile trail is on abandoned rail corridor
Surface: Original ballast

Contact:
Dave Hrdlicka
Forest Technician
White Mountain National Forest
Pemigewassett Ranger District
RFD 3, Box 15
Plymouth, NH 03264
(603)536-1310

⑬ Mason Railroad Trail

Endpoints: Wilton to Townsend, MA
Location: Hillsborough and Middlesex Counties
Length: 6.7 miles
Surface: Original ballast

Contact:
Liz Fletcher
Commissioner
Mason Conservation Commission
Mann House
Darling Hill Road
Mason, NH 03048
(603)878-2070

⑭ Moriah Brook Trail

Endpoints: White Mountain National Forest
Location: Coos County
Length: 3.0 miles of 5.3-mile trail is on abandoned rail corridor
Surface: Gravel and dirt

Contact:
Terri Marceron
Assistant Ranger
White Mountain National Forest
Androscoggin Ranger District
80 Glen Road
Gorham, NH 03581
(603)466-2713

⑮ North Twin Trail

Endpoints: White Mountain National Forest
Location: Grafton County
Length: 1.9 miles of 4.3-mile trail is on abandoned rail corridor
Surface: Dirt

Contact:
Roger Collins
Forest Technician
White Mountain National Forest
P.O. Box 239
Bethlehem, NH 03574-0239
(603)869-2626

⑯ Oliverian Trail

Endpoints: White Mountain National Forest
Location: Carroll County
Length: 0.5 miles of 3.5-mile trail is on abandoned rail corridor
Surface: Dirt

 on certain sections

Contact:
Eric Swett
Forest Technician
White Mountain National Forest
Saco Ranger District
33 Kancamagus Highway
Conway, NH 03818
(603)447-5448

⓱ Osseo Trail

Endpoints: White Mountain National Forest
Location: Grafton County
Length: 0.3 miles of 5.8-mile trail is on abandoned rail corridor
Surface: Dirt

Contact:
Dave Hrdlicka
Forest Technician
White Mountain National Forest
Pemigewassett Ranger District
RFD 3, Box 15
Plymouth, NH 03264
(603)536-1310

⓲ Pine Bend Brook Trail

Endpoints: White Mountain National Forest
Location: Carroll County
Length: 0.3 miles of 4.3-mile trail is on abandoned rail corridor
Surface: Gravel

Contact:
Eric Swett
Forest Technician
White Mountain National Forest
Saco Ranger District
33 Kancamagus Highway
Conway, NH 03818
(603)447-5448

⓳ Rob Brook Trail

Endpoints: White Mountain National Forest
Location: Carroll County
Length: 1.2 miles of 2.0-mile trail is on abandoned rail corridor
Surface: Original ballast

Contact:
Eric Swett
Forest Technician
White Mountain National Forest
Saco Ranger District
33 Kancamagus Highway
Conway, NH 03818
(603)447-5448

⓴ Rockingham Recreational Trail

Endpoints: Manchester to Newfields
Location: Hillsborough and Rockingham Counties
Length: 28.0 miles
Surface: Original ballast

Contact:
Paul Gray
Chief of Trails Bureau
Department of Resources and Economic Development
Division of Parks and Recreation
P.O. Box 856
Concord, NH 03302-0856
(603)271-3254

㉑ Rocky Branch Trail

Endpoints: White Mountain National Forest
Location: Carroll County
Length: 6.0 miles of 9.0-mile trail is on abandoned rail corridor
Surface: Original ballast

Contact:
Eric Swett
Forest Technician
White Mountain National Forest
Saco Ranger District
33 Kancamagus Highway
Conway, NH 03818
(603)447-5448

㉒ Sawyer River Trail

Endpoints: White Mountain National Forest
Location: Carroll County
Length: 4.0 miles
Surface: Original ballast

 on certain sections

Contact:
Eric Swett
Forest Technician
White Mountain National Forest
Saco Ranger District
33 Kancamagus Highway
Conway, NH 03818
(603)447-5448

㉓ Shelburne Trail

Endpoints: White Mountain National Forest
Location: Coos County
Length: 1.0 mile of 7.2-mile trail is on abandoned rail corridor
Surface: Dirt

Contact:
Terri Marceron
Assistant Ranger
White Mountain National Forest
Androscoggin Ranger District
80 Glen Road
Gorham, NH 03581
(603)466-2713

㉔ Spider Bridge Loop Trail

Endpoints: White Mountain National Forest
Location: Coos County
Length: 2.7 miles of 4.5-mile trail is on abandoned rail corridor
Surface: Gravel

Contact:
Katherine Bulchis
District Ranger
White Mountain National Forest
Androscoggin Ranger District
80 Glen Road
Gorham, NH 03581-1322
(603)466-2713

㉕ Sugar River Recreation Trail

Endpoints: Newport to Claremont
Location: Sullivan County
Length: 8.0 miles
Surface: Gravel and original ballast

Contact:
Robert Spoerl
Program Specialist
NH Division of Parks & Recreation, Trails Bureau
172 Pembroke Road
P.O. Box 1856
Concord, NH 03302-1856
(603)271-3254

㉖ Thoreau Falls Trail

Endpoints: White Mountain National Forest
Location: Grafton County
Length: 3.8 miles of 5.1-mile trail is on abandoned rail corridor
Surface: Original ballast

Contact:
Dave Hrdlicka
Forest Technician
White Mountain National Forest
Pemigewassett Ranger District
RFD 3, Box 15
Plymouth, NH 03264
(306)536-1310

㉗ Trestle Trail

Endpoints: White Mountain National Forest
Location: Coos County
Length: 0.2 miles of 1.0-mile trail is on abandoned rail corridor
Surface: Dirt

Contact:
Roger Collins
Forest Technician
White Mountain National Forest
P.O. Box 239
Bethlehem, NH 03574-0239
(603)869-2626

㉘ Upper Nanamocomuck Trail

Endpoints: White Mountain National Forest
Location: Carroll County
Length: 2.0 miles of 9.3-mile trail is on abandoned rail corridor
Surface: Original ballast

Contact:
Eric Swett
Forest Technician
White Mountain National Forest
Saco Ranger District
33 Kancamagus Highway
Conway, NH 03818
(603)447-5448

㉙ West Milan Trail

Endpoints: White Mountain National Forest
Location: Coos County
Length: 4.5 miles
Surface: Gravel

Contact:
Katherine Bulchis
District Ranger
White Mountain National Forest
Androscoggin Ranger District
80 Glen Road
Gorham, NH 03581-1322
(603)466-2713

㉚ Wild River Trail

Endpoints: White Mountain National Forest
Location: Coos County
Length: 4.5 miles
Surface: Gravel and dirt

Contact:
Terri Marceron
Assistant Ranger
White Mountain National Forest
Androscoggin Ranger District
80 Glen Road
Gorham, NH 03581
(603)466-2713

㉛ Wilderness Trail

Endpoints: White Mountain National Forest
Location: Grafton County
Length: 8.9 miles
Surface: Original ballast and dirt

Contact:
Dave Hrdlicka
Forest Technician
White Mountain National Forest
Pemigewassett Ranger District
RD 3, Box 15
Plymouth, NH 30264
(603)536-1310

㉜ Wolfeboro–Sanbornville Recreational Trail

Endpoints: Wolfeboro Falls to Sanbornville
Location: Carroll County
Length: 11.0 mile
Surface: Gravel and dirt

Contacts:
Town of Wolfeboro
P.O. Box 629
Wolfeboro, NH 03894
(603)569-5639

Paul Gray
Chief of Trails Bureau
Department of Resources and Economic Development
Division of Parks and Recreation
P.O. Box 856
Concord, NH 03302-0856
(603)271-3254

㉝ York Pond Trail

Endpoints: White Mountain National Forest
Location: Coos County
Length: 2.5 miles of 6.5-mile trail is on abandoned rail corridor
Surface: Dirt

Contact:
Katherine Bulchis
District Ranger
White Mountain National Forest
Androscoggin Ranger District
80 Glen Road
Gorham, NH 03581-1322
(603)466-2713

㉞ Zealand Trail

Endpoints: White Mountain National Forest
Location: Grafton County
Length: 2.5 miles
Surface: Dirt

Contact:
Roger Collins
Forest Technician
White Mountain National Forest
P.O. Box 239
Bethlehem, NH 03574-0239
(603)869-2626

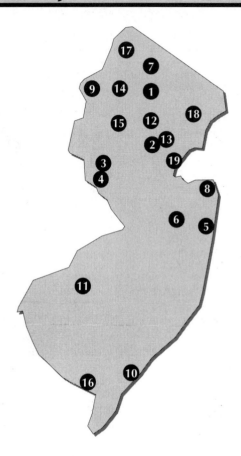

➋ Black River Wildlife Management Area Trail

Endpoints: Chester
Location: Morris County
Length: 4.0 miles
Surface: Original ballast

Contact:
Black River Wildlife
Management Area
275 North Road
Chester, NJ 07930
(908)879-6252

➌ Capoolong Creek Wildlife Management Area

Endpoints: Pittstown to
Landsdown
Location: Hunterdon
County
Length: 3.7 miles
Surface: Cinder

Contact:
Joseph Penkala
Regional Supervisor
New Jersey Division of Fish,
Game and Wildlife
150 Fradon-Springdale Road
Newton, NJ 07860-9639
(908)735-8793

➊ Berkshire Valley Management Area Trail

Endpoints: Lake
Hopatcong
Location: Morris County
Length: 3.0 miles
Surface: Original ballast

Contact:
John Piccolo
Black River Wildlife
Management Area
275 North Road
Chester, NJ 07930
(908)879-6252

❹ Delaware and Raritan Canal State Park Trail

Endpoints: Ewing to Milford and Trenton to New Brunswick
Location: Hunterdon, Mercer and Somerset Counties
Length: 32.0 miles of 68.0-mile trail is on abandoned rail corridor
Surface: Crushed stone and gravel

  on certain sections

Contact:
Paul Stern, Superintendent
Delaware and Raritan Canal
State Park Trail
643 Canal Road
Somerset, NJ 08873-7309
(908)873-3050

❺ Edgar Felix Memorial Bikeway

Endpoints: Manasquan to Allaire State Park
Location: Monmouth County
Length: 3.6 miles
Surface: Asphalt

Contact:
Thomas White, Director
Wall Township Parks &
Recreation
2700 Allaire Road
Wall, NJ 07719
(908)449-8444

❻ Freehold and Jamesburg Railroad Trail

Endpoints: Allaire State Park
Location: Monmouth County
Length: 3.0 miles of 4.5-mile trail is on abandoned rail corridor
Surface: Dirt

Contact:
Nick DeMicco
Superintendent
Allaire State Park
P.O. Box 220
Farmingdale, NJ 07727
(908)938-2371

❼ Hamburg Mountain Wildlife Management Area

Endpoints: Ogdensburg to Franklin
Location: Sussex County
Length: 3.0 miles
Surface: Original ballast

Contact:
Joseph Penkala
Regional Supervisor
NJ Division of Fish, Game
& Wildlife
150 Fradon-Springdale Road
Newton, NJ 07860-9639
(908)735-8793

❽ Henry Hudson Trail

Endpoints: Aberdeen Township to Leonardo
Location: Monmouth County
Length: 9.2 miles
Surface: Asphalt, crushed stone and wood chips

Contact:
Faith Hahn
Supervising Planner
Monmouth County Park
System
Public Information Office
805 Newman Springs Road
Lincroft, NJ 07738-1695
(908)842-4000

❾ Karamac Trail

Endpoints: Worthington State Forest
Location: Warren County
Length: 2.0 miles
Surface: Cinder

Contact:
Ed Pomeroy, Chief Ranger
Worthington State Forest
HC 62, Box 2
Columbia, NJ 07832
(908)841-9575

⑩ Linwood Bikepath

Endpoints: Linwood
Location: Atlantic County
Length: 1.8 miles
Surface: Asphalt

Contact:
Gary Gardner, City Clerk
Linwood City Hall
400 Poplar Avenue
Linwood, NJ 08221
(609)927-4108

⑪ Monroe Township Bikepath

Endpoints: Williamstown
Location: Gloucester County
Length: 1.5 miles
Surface: Asphalt

Contact:
Deborah Terch
Community Affairs Director
Monroe Township Dept. of
Parks & Recreation
Pfeiffer Community Center
301 Bluebell Road
Williamstown, NJ 08094
(609)728-9823

⑫ Ogden Mine Railroad Path

Endpoints: Hurdtown
Location: Morris and
Sussex Counties
Length: 2.5 miles
Surface: Original ballast

Contact:
Albert Kent
Morris County Park
Commission
P.O. Box 1295
Morristown, NJ 17962-1295
(201)326-7600

⑬ Patriots' Path

Endpoints: East Hanover
to Washington
Location: Morris County
Length: 7.0 miles of 12.0-
mile trail is on abandoned
rail corridor
Surface: Asphalt, gravel
and dirt

 on certain
sections

Contact:
Al Kent, Commissioner
Morris County Park
Commission
P.O. Box 1295
Morristown, NJ 07962-1295
(201)326-7600

⑭ Paulinskill Valley Trail

Endpoints: Sparta Junction
Location: Sussex and
Warren Counties
Length: 27.0 miles
Surface: Dirt and cinder

Contact:
Park Superintendent
Kittatinny Valley State Park
P.O. Box 621
Andover, NJ 07821
(201)786-6445

⑮ Pequest Wildlife Management Area Trail

Endpoints: Pequest
Location: Warren County
Length: 4.2 miles
Surface: Crushed stone

Contact:
Black River Wildlife
Management Area
275 North Road
Chester, NJ 07930
(908)879-6252

⑯ Seashore Line Trail

Endpoints: Belleplain
State Forest
Location: Cape May and
Cumberland Counties
Length: 10.0 miles
Surface: Original ballast
and dirt

Contact:
Tom Keck
Superintendent
Belleplain State Forest
Route 550, Box 450
Woodbine, NJ 08270-0450
(609)861-2404

⑰ Sussex Branch Railroad Trail

Endpoints: Byram Township to Branchville
Location: Sussex County
Length: 21.2 miles
Surface: Original ballast and cinder

Contact:
Park Superintendent
Kittatinny Valley State Park
P.O. Box 621
Andover, NJ 07821
(201)786-6445

⑱ Traction Line Recreation Trail

Endpoints: Morristown to Madison
Location: Morris County
Length: 2.0 miles (will be 2.9 miles when completed)
Surface: Asphalt

Contact:
Al Kent, Commissioner
Morris County Park Commission
P.O. Box 1295
Morristown, NJ 07962-1295
(201)326-7600

⑲ West Essex Bike Path

Endpoints: Little Falls to Cedar Grove
Location: Essex County
Length: 2.2 miles
Surface: Gravel and cinder

Contact:
Vincent Burci
Chief Engineer
Essex County Department of Parks
115 Clifton Avenue
Newark, NJ 07104
(201)268-3500

NEW MEXICO

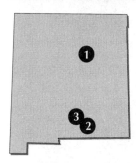

❶ Gillinas Hiking Trail

Endpoints: Las Vegas
Location: San Miguel County
Length: 1.5 miles (will be 7.0 miles when completed)
Surface: Asphalt

Contact:
Orlando Brown, Director
Recreation Department
P.O. Box 179
Las Vegas, NM 87701
(505)454-1158

❷ Grandview Trail

Endpoints: Lincoln National Forest
Location: Otero County
Length: 1.6 miles of 1.7-mile trail is on abandoned rail corridor
Surface: Original ballast

Contact:
Johnny Wilson
Staff Officer
Lincoln National Forest
1101 New York Avenue
Alamagordo, NM 88310
(505)437-7200

❸ Mexican Canyon Trestle Trail

Endpoints: Lincoln National Forest
Location: Otero County
Length: 1.0 mile of 2.4-mile trail is on abandoned rail corridor
Surface: Original ballast

Contact:
Johnny Wilson
Staff Officer
Lincoln National Forest
1101 New York Avenue
Alamagordo, NM 88310
(505)437-7200

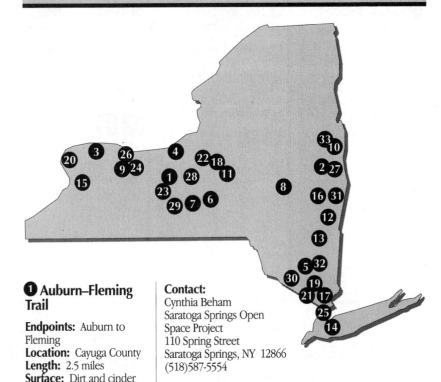

❶ Auburn–Fleming Trail

Endpoints: Auburn to Fleming
Location: Cayuga County
Length: 2.5 miles
Surface: Dirt and cinder

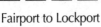

Contact:
Tom Higgins
County Planner
Cayuga County Planning Board
160 Genesee Street
Auburn, NY 13021-3424
(315)253-1276

❷ Bog Meadow Brook Trail

Endpoints: Saratoga Springs
Location: Saratoga County
Length: 2.0 miles
Surface: Original ballast

Contact:
Cynthia Beham
Saratoga Springs Open Space Project
110 Spring Street
Saratoga Springs, NY 12866
(518)587-5554

❸ Canalway Trail

Location: Cayuga, Monroe, Niagara, Onondaga and Orleans Counties
Length: 95.0 miles open in two separate sections

Contact:
John DiMurra
Project Manager
New York State Thruway Authority
200 Southern Blvd.
Albany, NY 12209
(518)436-3034

Camillus to Port Byron Section

Endpoints: Camillus to Port Byron
Length: 20.0 miles
Surface: Dirt

Fairport to Lockport Section

Endpoints: Fairport to Lockport
Length: 75.0 miles
Surface: Asphalt, crushed stone and dirt

 on certain sections

❹ Cayuga County Trail

Endpoints: Cato to Fair Haven
Location: Cayuga County
Length: 15.0 miles
Surface: Dirt and cinder

Contact:
Tom Higgins
County Planner
Cayuga County Planning Board
160 Genesee Street
Auburn, NY 13021-3424
(315)253-1276

❺ D&H Canal Heritage Corridor

Endpoints: Kingston to Spring Glen
Location: Ulster County
Length: 12.0 miles of 19.0-mile trail is on abandoned rail corridor (will be 30.0 miles when completed)
Surface: Crushed stone and cinder

Contact:
Sheldon Quimby
P.O. Box 362
Port Ewen, NY 12466
(914)339-4531

❻ Dryden Lake Park Trail

Endpoints: Dryden
Location: Tompkins County
Length: 3.3 miles (will be 5.3 miles when completed)
Surface: Original ballast and grass

Contacts:
Candice Cornell
Tompkins County Greenway Coalition
1456 Hanshaw Road
Ithaca, NY 14850
(607)257-6220

Jim Shugg
Supervisor
Town of Dryden
65 East Main St.
Dryden, NY 13053
(607)844-8619

❼ East Ithaca Recreation Way

Endpoints: Ithaca
Location: Tompkins County
Length: 2.2 miles
Surface: Gravel and grass

Contact:
Richard Schoch, Manager
Ithaca Parks and Open Space
106 Seven Mile Drive
Ithaca, NY 14850-8747
(607)273-8035

❽ Erie Canal Trail

Endpoints: Amsterdam to Schoharie State Park
Location: Schenectady County
Length: 8.0 miles of 90.0-mile trail is on abandoned rail corridor
Surface: Asphalt

Contact:
Janice Fontanella
Site Manager
Schoharie Crossing State Historic Site
P.O. Box 140
Fort Hunter, NY 12069-0140
(518)829-7516

❾ Genesee Valley Greenway

Endpoints: Rochester to Portageville
Location: Allegany, Genesee, Livingston, Monroe and Wyoming Counties
Length: 7 miles (will be 50 miles when completed)
Surface: Gravel and grass

Contacts:
Fran Gotshik
Local Greenway Coordinator
NY Parks and Conservation Association
46 Prince Street
Rochester, NY 14607-1090
(716)624-2484

Joe Regal
Friends of the Genesee Valley Greenway
39 Murray Street
Mt. Morris, NY 11410
(716)658-3174

❿ Glens Falls Feeder Canal Trail

Endpoints: Glens Falls to Ft. Edward
Location: Warren County
Length: 9.0 miles
Surface: Crushed stone

Contact:
John DiMura
Project Manager
New York Thruway Authority
200 Southern Blvd.
Albany, NY 12209
(518)436-3034

⓫ Gorge Trail

Endpoints: Cazenovia
Location: Madison County
Length: 2.2 miles
Surface: Crushed stone and original ballast

Contact:
Richard Paluseo
Cazenovia Preservation Foundation
P.O. Box 432
Cazenovia, NY 13035
(315)655-3105

⓬ Harlem Valley Rail Trail

Endpoints: Chatham to Wassaic
Location: Columbia and Dutchess Counties
Length: 4 miles (will be 20 miles when completed)
Surface: Dirt

Contact:
Dutchess County Dept. of Parks, Rec. & Conservation
Bowdoin Park
85 Sheafe Road
Wappingers Falls, NY 12590
(914)297-1224

⓭ Hojack Trail

Endpoints: Redcreek to Hannibal
Location: Cayuga, Monroe, Niagara, Orleans, Oswego and Wayne Counties
Length: 8 miles (will be 160 miles when completed)
Surface: Dirt and cinder

Contact:
Tom Higgins
County Planner
Cayuga County Planning Board
160 Genesee Street
Auburn, NY 13021-3424
(315)253-1276

⓮ John Kieran Nature Trail

Endpoints: Bronx
Location: Bronx County
Length: 0.3 miles of 1.0-mile trail is on abandoned rail corridor
Surface: Wood chips and dirt

Contact:
Marianne Anderson
Van Cortlandt and Pelham Bay Parks Administration
1 Bronx River Parkway
Bronx, NY 10462
(718)430-1890

⓯ Lehigh Memory Trail

Endpoints: Williamsville
Location: Erie County
Length: 0.7 miles
Surface: Asphalt

Contact:
Barbara Schofield, Trustee
Village of Williamsville
P.O. Box 155
Williamsville, NY 14231-1557
(716)632-4120

Mohawk-Hudson Bikeway

Endpoints: Albany to Rotterdam Junction
Location: Albany and Schenectady Counties
Length: 19.5 miles of 41.0-mile trail is on abandoned rail corridor
Surface: Asphalt and crushed stone

Albany Section

Contact:
Mark King
Albany County Planning Department
112 State Street, Room 1006
Albany, NY 12207-2005
(518)447-5660

Colonie Section

Contact:
James Zambardino
Superintendent
Colonie Recreation and Parks Department
89 Schermerhorn Road
Cohoes, NY 12047-0442
(518)783-2760

Niskayuna Section

Contact:
Edwin Reilly, Supervisor
Town of Niskayuna
1335 Balltown Road
Schenectady, NY 12309
(518)374-7710

Rotterdam Section

Contact:
Denise Cahsmere
Senior Planner
Schenectady County Planning Dept.
1 Broadway Center
Suite 800
Schenectady, NY 12305
(518)386-2225

Schenectady Section

Contact:
William Seber, Director
Department of Parks & Recreation
City Hall
Jay Street
Schenectady, NY 12305
(518)386-2225

North County Trailway

Endpoints: Eastview to Hawthorne; Briarcliff to Law Memorial Park; Mt. Plesant to Kitchiawan
Location: Westchester County
Length: 12.0 miles of 15.0-mile trail is on abandoned rail corridor
Surface: Asphalt

Contact:
David DeLucia
Director of Park Facilities
Westchester County Parks & Recreation
19 Bradhurst Avenue
Hawthorne, NY 10532
(914)593-2600

 Old Erie Canal State Park

Endpoints: Dewitt to Rome
Location: Madison, Oneida and Onondaga Counties
Length: 46.0 miles
Surface: Crushed stone

Contact:
Kenneth Showalter
Park Manager
Old Erie Canal State Park
NYS Office of Parks, Rec. & Historic Preservation
Andrus Road
Kirkville, NY 13082
(315)687-7821

Old Mine Railroad Trail

Endpoints: Fahnestock State Park
Location: Putnam County
Length: 2.2 miles
Surface: Dirt

Contact:
Jane Daniels
East Hudson Trails Chair
New York-New Jersey Trail Conference
232 Madison Avenue
New York, NY 10016

⑳ Ongiara Trail System

Endpoints: Whirlpool State Park to Devil's Hole State Park
Location: Niagara County
Length: 1.1 miles
Surface: Crushed stone

Contact:
Bill Huntoon, Park Manager
New York State Parks —
Niagara Region
Niagara Reservation
P.O. Box 1132
Niagara Falls, NY 14303-0132
(716)285-3891

㉑ Orange Heritage Trail

Endpoints: Goshen
Location: Orange County
Length: 2.5 miles
Surface: Crushed stone and original ballast

Contact:
Graham Skea
Commissioner
Orange County Dept. of
Parks, Recreation &
Conservation
550 Route 416
Montgomery, NY 12549
(914)457-3111

㉒ Oswego Recreational Trail

Endpoints: Fulton to Cleveland
Location: Oswego County
Length: 26.0 miles
Surface: Original ballast

 on certain sections

Contact:
Darrell Kehoe, Crew Leader
Oswego County Highway
Department
46 East Bridge Street
Oswego, NY 13126-2123
(315)349-8331

㉓ Outlet Trail

Endpoints: Penn Yan to Dresden
Location: Yates County
Length: 7.5 miles
Surface: Asphalt and original ballast

Contact:
Virginia Gibbs
County Historian
110 Court Street, Room 3
Penn Yan, NY 14527-1130
(315)536-5147

㉔ Pittsford Trail System

Endpoints: Pittsford
Location: Monroe County
Length: 4.0 miles
Surface: Crushed stone and original ballast

Contact:
Doug Morgenfeld, Director
Pittsford Parks and Rec.
35 Lincoln Ave
Pittsford, NY 14534-1923
(716)248-6280

㉕ Raymond G. Esposito Trail

Endpoints: South Nyack
Location: Rockland County
Length: 1.0 mile
Surface: Crushed stone, gravel and dirt

Contact:
Mary Radich
Deputy Village Clerk
Village of South Nyack
282 South Broadway
South Nyack, NY 10960
(914)358-0287

㉖ Rochester, Syracuse and Eastern Trail

Endpoints: Perinton to Fairport
Location: Monroe County
Length: 6.0 miles
Surface: Crushed stone

Contact:
David Morgan
Director of Parks
Town of Perinton
1350 Turk Hill Road
Fairport, NY 14450-8751
(716)223-5050

27 Saratoga Springs Bicycle/Pedestrian Path

Endpoints: Saratoga Springs
Location: Saratoga County
Length: 0.6 miles
Surface: Asphalt

Contact:
Cynthia Beham
Saratoga Springs Open
Space Project
110 Spring Street
Saratoga Springs, NY 12866
(518)587-5554

28 Skaneateles Nature Trail

Endpoints: Skaneateles
Location: Onondaga County
Length: 2.0 miles (will be 4.0 miles when completed)
Surface: Dirt

Contact:
Matthew Major, Supervisor
Town of Skaneateles
Recreation Dept.
24 Jordan Street
Skaneateles, NY 13152-1110
(315)685-5607

29 South Hill Recreation Way

Endpoints: Ithaca
Location: Tompkins County
Length: 3.0 miles of 3.3-mile trail is on abandoned rail corridor
Surface: Crushed stone and grass

Contacts:
Candice Cornell
Tompkins County
Greenway Coalition
1456 Hanshaw Road
Ithaca, NY 14850
(607)257-6220

George Frantz
Assistant Town Planner
Town of Ithaca
123 East Seneca Street
Ithaca, NY 14850
(607)273-1747

30 Sullivan County Rail-Trail

Endpoints: Westbrookville to Wurtsboro and Mountaindale to Woodbridge
Location: Sullivan County
Length: 14.0 miles
Surface: Gravel and dirt

Contact:
Dennis Houston
Sullivan County Rails-to-Trails Conservancy, Inc.
195 Lake Louise Marie Road
Rock Hill, NY 12715
(914)796-2100

31 Uncle Sam Bikeway

Endpoints: Troy
Location: Rensselaer County
Length: 3.5 miles
Surface: Asphalt

Contact:
Robert Weaver
Deputy Commissioner
Troy Parks & Recreation
Department
1 Monument Square
Troy, NY 12180-3212
(518)235-8993

32 Wallkill Valley Rail-Trail

Endpoints: Springtown to Gardiner
Location: Ulster County
Length: 12.2 miles (will be 15.2 miles when completed)
Surface: Original ballast

Contact:
Roland Bahret
Wallkill Valley Rail Trail
Association, Inc.
P.O. Box 1048
New Paltz, NY 12561-0020
(914)255-1436

③ Warren County Bikeway

Endpoints: Lake George to Glens Falls
Location: Warren County
Length: 7.0 miles of 11.0-mile trail is on abandoned rail corridor
Surface: Asphalt

Contact:
Patrick Beland
Trails Supervisor
Warren County Parks and
Rec. Dept.
261 Main Street
Warrensburg, NY 12885
(518)623-5576

NORTH CAROLINA

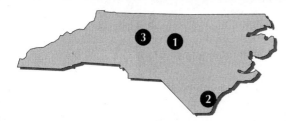

❶ Libba Cotton Trail

Endpoints: Carrboro
Location: Orange County
Length: 0.5 miles
Surface: Asphalt

Contact:
Roy Williford
Coordinator
Planning and Economic
Development
P.O. Box 829
Carrboro, NC 27510-0829
(919)968-7714

❷ River to Sea Bikeway

Endpoints: Wilmington to
Wrightsville Beach
Location: New Hanover
County
Length: 8.0 miles of 12.0-
mile trail is on abandoned
rail corridor
Surface: Asphalt and
concrete

Contact:
Joseph Huegy
Transportation Planner
City of Wilmington
P.O. Box 1810
Wilmington, NC 28402-1810
(919)341-7888

❸ Strollway

Endpoints: Winston-Salem
Location: Forsyth County
Length: 1.2 miles
Surface: Crushed stone

Contact:
Jack Steelman
Winston-Salem
Development Office
P.O. Box 2511
Winston-Salem, NC 27102
(919)727-2741

NORTH DAKOTA

❶ Roughrider Trail

Endpoints: Mandan to
Fort Rice
Location: Morton County
Length: 17.0 miles of 22.0-
mile trail is on abandoned
rail corridor
Surface: Gravel and dirt

Contact:
Bob Smith
State Trail Coordinator
Snowmobile North Dakota
1835 Bismarck Expressway
Bismarck, ND 58504
(701)328-5357

OHIO

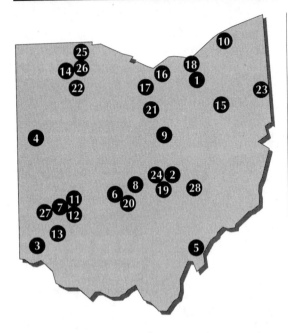

Contacts:
William Daehler
Planning Administrator
Office of Real Estate and
Land Management
Ohio Department of
Natural Resources
C-4, Fountain Square
Columbus, OH 43224
(614)265-6395

Greg Seymour
Preserve Manager
Blackhand Gorge Nature
Preserve
5213 Rockhaven Road, SE
Newark, OH 43055
(614)763-4411

❶ Bike and Hike Trail

Endpoints: Walton Hills to Kent and Stow
Location: Cuyahoga, Portage and Summit Counties
Length: 26.0 miles of 29.0-mile trail is on abandoned rail corridor
Surface: Asphalt and crushed stone

Akron Metroparks Section

Contact:
Thomas Shuster
Director
Summit County Metroparks
975 Treaty Line Road
Akron, OH 44313-5898
(216)867-5511

Cleveland Metroparks Section

Contact:
Stephen Coles
Chief of Park Planning
Cleveland Metroparks
4101 Fulton Parkway
Cleveland, OH 44144-1923
(216)351-6300

❷ Blackhand Gorge Bikeway

Endpoints: Blackhand Gorge Nature Preserve
Location: Licking County
Length: 4.0 miles
Surface: Asphalt

❸ California Junction Trail

Endpoints: California Woods Nature Preserve
Location: Hamilton County
Length: 0.8 miles of 1.0-mile trail is on abandoned rail corridor
Surface: Original ballast and wood chips

Contact:
James Farsing, Director of Education Services
California Woods Environmental Recreation Center
5400 Kellogg Avenue
Cincinnati, OH 45228-1007
(513)231-8678

88

❹ Celina-Coldwater Bikeway

Endpoints: Celina to Coldwater
Location: Mercer County
Length: 4.6 miles
Surface: Asphalt

Contact:
Mike Sovinski
Celina Engineering Dept.
426 West Market Street
Celina, OH 45822-2127
(419)586-1144

❺ Gallipolis Bike Path

Location: Gallia County
Length: 7 miles open in two separate sections (will be 22 miles when completed)

Contact:
Josette Baker, Director
O.O. McIntyre Park District
Gallia County Court House
18 Locust Street
Gallipolis, OH 45631-1251
(614)446-4612

Gallipolis to Spring Valley Section

Endpoints: Gallipolis to Spring Valley
Length: 2.5 miles (will be 19.5 miles when completed)
Surface: Crushed stone

Kerr to Bidwell Section

Endpoints: Kerr to Bidwell
Length: 4.5 miles
Surface: Crushed stone

❻ Heritage Trail

Endpoints: Hilliard
Location: Franklin County
Length: 1.5 miles (will be 7.5 miles when completed)
Surface: Asphalt

Contact:
Janell Thomas, Director
Parks & Recreation
Washington Township
4675 Cosgray Rd
Amlin, OH 43002-9786
(614)876-9554

❼ Huffman Prairie Overlook Trail

Endpoints: Bath Township
Location: Greene County
Length: 3.0 miles (will be 5.5 miles when completed)
Surface: Grass

Contact:
Elwood Ensor
Miami Valley Regional Bicycle Committee
1304 Horizon Drive
Fairborn, OH 45324-5816
(513)882-6000

❽ Interstate-670 Bikeway

Endpoints: Columbus
Location: Franklin County
Length: 3.0 miles
Surface: Asphalt

Contact:
Dale Hooper
City of Columbus
Division of Traffic Engineering
109 North Front Street
Columbus, OH 43215
(614)645-7790

❾ Kokosing Gap Trail

Endpoints: Danville to Mt. Vernon
Location: Knox County
Length: 14.0 miles
Surface: Asphalt

Contact:
Phil Samuel, President
Kokosing Gap Trail
P.O. Box 129
Gambier, OH 43022-0129
(614)427-4509

❿ Lake County Greenway

Endpoints: Painesville to Lake County line
Location: Lake County
Length: 4.5 miles of 5.0-mile trail is on abandoned rail corridor
Surface: Original ballast

Contact:
Chuck Kenzig
Lake Metro Parks
11211 Spear Road
Concord Township, OH 44077
(800)227-7275

⓫ Little Miami Bike Route

Endpoints: Springfield
Location: Clark County
Length: 1.5 miles of 3.0-mile trail is on abandoned rail corridor
Surface: Asphalt

Contact:
Tim Smith, Director
Springfield Parks & Recreation
City Hall
76 East High Street
Springfield, OH 45502-1236
(513)324-7348

⓬ Little Miami Scenic Trail

Endpoints: Xenia to Yellow Springs
Location: Greene County
Length: 9.7 miles (will be 16.7 miles when completed)
Surface: Asphalt with parallel grass treadway

Contact:
Charles Dressler, Director
Greene County Park District
651 Dayton-Xenia Road
Xenia, OH 45385-2699
(513)376-7440

⓭ Little Miami State Park Trail

Endpoints: Millford to Xenia
Location: Clermont, Greene, Hamilton and Warren Counties
Length: 43 miles (will be 50 miles when completed)
Surface: Asphalt and original ballast with parallel dirt treadway

Contact:
Chuck Thiemann, Manager
Little Miami Scenic State Park
8570 East State Route 73
Waynesville, OH 45068-9719
(513)897-3055

⓮ Miami & Erie Canal

Location: Lucas and Miami Counties
Length: 9.0 miles open in two separate sections
Surface: Dirt

Cross Trace to Laramie Creek Section

Endpoints: Cross Trace to Laramie Creek
Length: 1.0 mile
Surface: Dirt

Contact:
John Neilson, Manager
Piqua Historical Area State Memorial
9845 North Hardin Road
Piqua, OH 45356-9707
(513)773-2522

Farnsworth to Providence Section

Endpoints: Farnsworth to Providence
Length: 8.0 miles
Surface: Dirt

Contact:
Tom Shumaker
or Chuck Zientek
Farnsworth Metroparks
8505 South River Road
Waterville, OH 43566
(419)878-7641

⓯ Nickelplate Trail

Endpoints: Louisville
Location: Stark County
Length: 1.5 miles of 3.0-mile trail is on abandoned rail corridor
Surface: Asphalt

Contact:
Darrin Metzger
Parks Supervisor
City of Louisville Parks Department
215 South Mill Street
Louisville, OH 44641
(216)875-5644

⓰ North Coast Inland Trail

Endpoints: Elyria to Kipton
Location: Lorain County
Length: 14.0 miles
Surface: Asphalt

Contact:
Dan Martin
Executive Director
Lorain County Metropolitan
Park District
12882 Diagonal Road
La Grange, OH 44050-9728
(216)458-5121

⓱ Oberlin Bike Path

Endpoints: Oberlin
Location: Lorain County
Length: 2.8 miles
Surface: Asphalt

Contact:
Ronald Twining, Director
Community Services
City of Oberlin
85 South Main Street
Oberlin, OH 44074
(216)775-1531

⓲ Ohio & Erie Towpath Trail

Endpoints: Cuyahoga
Valley National Recreation
Area
Location: Cuyahoga and
Summit Counties
Length: 20.0 miles
Surface: Crushed stone

 on certain sections

Contact:
Cuyahoga Valley National
Recreation Area
Canal Visitor Center
15617 Vaughn Road
Brecksville, OH 44141
(216)524-1497

⓳ Ohio Canal Greenway

Endpoints: Hebron to
Licking County line
Location: Licking County
Length: 2.8 miles
Surface: Crushed stone

Contact:
Russell Edington
Licking Park District
4309 Lancaster Road
Granville, OH 43023
(614)587-2535

⓴ Olentangy–Scioto Bike Path

Endpoints: Columbus
Location: Franklin County
Length: 1.5 miles of 18.0-mile trail is on abandoned rail corridor
Surface: Asphalt and concrete

Contact:
Mollie O'Donnell
Landscape Architect
City of Columbus
Recreation and Parks
Department
420 West Whittier Street
Columbus, OH 43215
(614)645-3300

㉑ Richland B&O Trail

Endpoints: Butler to
Mansfield
Location: Richland
County
Length: 18.0 miles
Surface: Asphalt

Contact:
Steve McKee, Director
Richland County Park
District
2295 Lexington Avenue
Mansfield, OH 44907-3027
(419)884-3764

㉒ Slippery Elm Trail

Endpoints: Bowling Green
to Baltimore
Location: Wood County
Length: 13.0 miles
Surface: Asphalt

Contact:
Andrew Kalmar, Director
Wood County Park District
18729 Mercer Road
Bowling Green, OH 43402
(419)353-1897

23 Stavich Bicycle Trail

Endpoints: Struthers to New Castle, PA
Location: Lawrence and Mahoning Counties
Length: 11.0 mile
Surface: Asphalt

Contact:
Gary Slaven
Falcon Foundry
6th and Water Street
Lowellville, OH 44436
(216)536-6221

24 Thomas J. Evans Bike Trail

Endpoints: Newark to Johnstown
Location: Licking County
Length: 14.5 miles
Surface: Asphalt

Contact:
Russell Edgington
Licking Park District
4309 Lancaster Road
Granville, OH 43023-9509
(614)587-2535

25 University–Parks Bike-Hike Trail

Endpoints: Toledo
Location: Lucas County
Length: 8.5 miles
Surface: Asphalt

Contact:
Jean Ward, Director
Toledo Area Metroparks
5100 West Central
Toledo, OH 43615
(419)535-3050

26 Wabash Cannonball Trail

Endpoints: Maumee to Montpelier
Location: Fulton, Henry, Lucas and Williams Counties
Length: 20.2 miles (will be 63 miles when completed)
Surface: Original ballast

Contact:
Gene Markley
Vice President
Northwestern Ohio Rails-to-Trails Association
P.O. Box 234
Delta, OH 43515
(419)822-4788

27 Wolf Creek Bikeway

Endpoints: Trotwood to Brookville
Location: Montgomery County
Length: 13.0 miles
Surface: Crushed stone

Contact:
Mark Giesel, Park Ranger
Five Rivers Metro Parks
1375 East Siebenthaler Avenue
Dayton, OH 45414-5398
(513)278-8231

28 Zanesville Riverfront Bikepath

Endpoints: Zanesville
Location: Muskingum County
Length: 2.9 miles
Surface: Asphalt

Contact:
Ernest Bynum
Recreation Director
City of Zanesville
401 Market Street
Zanesville, OH 43701-3520
(614)455-0609

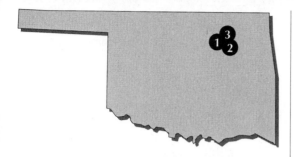

❸ Midland Valley Trail & River Parks Pedestrian Bridge

Endpoints: Tulsa
Location: Tulsa County
Length: 1.3 miles (will be 2.3 miles when completed)
Surface: Asphalt

Contact:
Jackie Bubenick
Executive Director
River Parks Authority
707 South Houston
Suite 202
Tulsa, OK 74127-9000
(918)596-2001

❶ Cleveland Trail

Endpoints: Cleveland
Location: Pawnee County
Length: 3.0 miles
Surface: Asphalt

Contact:
Eric Kuykendall
City Manager
City of Cleveland
105 North Division
Cleveland, OK 74020-3829
(918)358-3600

❷ Katy Trail

Endpoints: Kalamazoo to South Haven
Location: Tulsa County
Length: 11.0 mile
Surface: Asphalt

Contact:
Jackie Bubenick
Executive Director
River Parks Authority
707 South Houston
Suite 202
Tulsa, OK 74127-9000
(918)596-2001

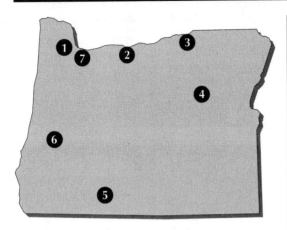

❶ Banks–Vernonia Linear Park

Endpoints: Banks to Vernonia
Location: Columbia County
Length: 21.0 mile
Surface: Gravel

Contact:
Jim Boder, Park Manager
Champoge State Park
7679 Champoge Road, NE
St. Paul, OR 97137
(503)633-8170

❷ Deshuttes River Trail

Endpoints: Deshuttes State Park
Location: Sherman County
Length: 17.0 miles
Surface: Dirt

Contacts:
Jennette Bondsteel
Park Manager
State & Recreation Area
89600 Biggs Rufus Highway
Wasco, OR 97065
(503)739-2322

Peter Bond
Trails Coordinator
Oregon Parks & Recreation Department
1115 Commercial Street, NE
Salem, OR 97310-1001
(503)378-5020

❸ Lake Wallula Scenic River Hiking Trail

Endpoints: Hat Rock State Park to McNary Beach Park
Location: Umatilla County
Length: 4.9 miles (will be 10.4 miles when completed)
Surface: Gravel

Contact:
Jeff Phillip
Park Ranger
Core of Engineers
McNary Dam
P.O. Box 1230
Umatilla, OR 97882
(503)922-3211

❹ Malheur Trail

Endpoints: Malheur National Forest
Location: Grant County
Length: 12.5 miles
Surface: Original ballast

Contact:
Tim Kimble
Recreation Staff Officer
Recreation Wilderness Trails
139 N.E. Dayton Street
John Day, OR 97845
(503)575-1731

❺ OC&E Rail-Trail State Park

Endpoints: Bly to Klamath Falls
Location: Klamath County
Length: 64.5 miles
Surface: Original ballast

Contact:
Park Manager
Collier State Park
4600 Highway 97-N
Chiloquin, OR 97624
(503)783-2471

❻ Row River Trail

Endpoints: Culp Creek to Cottage Grove
Location: Lane County
Length: 14.0 miles
Surface: Crushed stone

Contact:
Vicki Kellerman
Eugene District Bureau of Land Management
2890 Chad Drive
P.O. Box 10226
Eugene, OR 97440
(503)683-6600

❼ Springwater Trail Corridor

Endpoints: Boring to Portland
Location: Clackamas and Multnomah Counties
Length: 16.5 miles
Surface: Asphalt and gravel with parallel wood chip treadway

Contact:
George Hudson
Landscape Architect
City of Portland
Parks & Recreation Dept.
1122 S.W. 5th Avenue, Suite 1302
Portland, OR 97204-1933
(503)823-6183

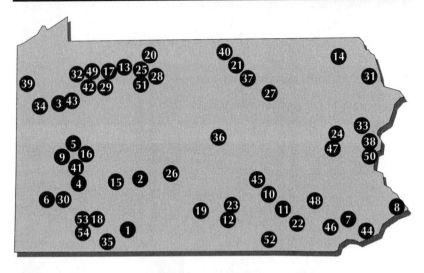

① Allegheny Highlands Trail

Endpoints: Garrett to Markleton
Location: Allegheny and Somerset Counties
Length: 46 miles (will be 60 miles when completed)
Surface: Crushed stone

Contact:
Hank Parke, President
Somerset County Rails-to-Trails
829 North Central Avenue
Somerset, PA 15501-1029
(814)445-6431

② Allegheny Portage Railroad Trails

Endpoints: Allegheny Portage RR National Historic Site
Location: Blair and Cambria Counties
Length: 1.5 miles of 7.0-mile trail is on abandoned rail corridor
Surface: Original ballast, grass and wood chips

Contact:
Gary Traynham
Unit Manager
Allegheny Portage RR National Historic Site
P.O. Box 189
Cresson, PA 16630
(814)886-6150

③ Allegheny River Trail

Endpoints: Brandon to Franklin
Location: Venango County
Length: 11 miles (will be 14 miles when completed)
Surface: Asphalt and crushed stone with parallel dirt treadway

Contact:
James Holden
or Neal Parker
Allegheny Valley Trails Association
Franklin Area Chamber of Commerce
1256 Liberty Street, Suite 2
Franklin, PA 16323
(814)437-5621

❹ Arboretum Trail

Endpoints: Oakmont
Location: Allegheny County
Length: 1.0 mile
Surface: Asphalt

Contact:
Kitty Vagley, Director
Garden Club
830 15th Street
Oakmont, PA 15139
(412)828-5203

❺ Armstrong Trail

Endpoints: Schenley to Upper Hillville
Location: Armstrong and Clarion Counties
Length: 52.5 miles
Surface: Gravel and original ballast

Contact:
Susan Torrence
Armstrong County Tourist Bureau
402 East Market Street
Kittaning, PA 16201-1409
(412)548-3226

❻ Arrowhead Trail

Endpoints: McMurray
Location: Washington County
Length: 3.5 miles (will be 6.0 miles when completed)
Surface: Asphalt and original ballast

Contact:
Joanne Nelson, Director
Peters Township
Department of Parks and Recreation
610 E. McMurray Road
McMurray, PA 15317-3420
(412)942-5000

❼ Betzwood Rail Trail

Endpoints: Valley Forge National Historic Park
Location: Montgomery County
Length: 2.0 miles
Surface: Original ballast

Contact:
Scott Kalbach
Chief Park Ranger
Valley Forge National Historic Park
P.O. Box 953
Valley Forge, PA 19481
(610)783-1046

❽ Bristol Spurline Park

Endpoints: Bristol
Location: Bucks County
Length: 1.5 miles (will be 2.0 miles when completed)
Surface: Asphalt

Contact:
Fidel Esposito, Manager
Borough of Bristol
250 Pond Street
Bristol, PA 19007-4937
(215)788-3828

❾ Butler–Freeport Community Trail

Endpoints: Butler to Freeport
Location: Armstrong and Butler Counties
Length: 12 miles (will be 20.7 miles when completed)
Surface: Crushed stone and original ballast

Contact:
Ron Bennett, President
Butler-Freeport Community Trail Council
P.O. Box 533
Saxonburg, PA 16056-0533
(412)352-4783

❿ City Island Foot Bridge

Endpoints: Harrisburg
Location: Dauphin County
Length: 1.0 mile
Surface: Asphalt

Contact:
Tina Manoogian-King
Director
Harrisburg Parks & Recreation
10 North Second Street, Suite 401
Harrisburg, PA 17101-1686
(717)255-3020

⓫ Conewago Trail

Endpoints: Elizabethtown to Lebanon County line
Location: Lancaster County
Length: 5.0 miles
Surface: Dirt and cinder

Contact:
John Gerencser
Recreation Coordinator
Lancaster County Parks & Recreation
1050 Rockford Road
Lancaster, PA 17602-4624
.(717)299-8215

⓬ Cumberland County Biker/Hiker Trail

Endpoints: Pine Grove Furnace State Park
Location: Cumberland County
Length: 5.3 miles of 5.5-mile trail is on abandoned rail corridor
Surface: Crushed stone

Contact:
Bill Rosevear, Park Manager
Pine Grove Furnace
State Park
1100 Pine Grove Road
Gardeners, PA 17324
(717)486-7174

⓭ Deerlick Cross-Country Ski Trail

Endpoints: Allegheny National Forest
Location: Warren County
Length: 2.0 miles of 9.0-mile trail is on abandoned rail corridor
Surface: Original ballast, grass and dirt

Contact:
Karen Mollander
District Ranger
Allegheny National Forest
Sheffield Ranger District
Route 6
Sheffield, PA 16347
(814)968-3232

⓮ Endless Mountains Riding Trail

Endpoints: Alford to Montrose
Location: Susquehanna County
Length: 14.0 miles
Surface: Original ballast

Contact:
Anne Bensch, President
Bridgewater Riding Club
P.O. Box 27
South Montrose, PA 18843
(717)278-1454

⓯ Ghost Town Trail

Endpoints: Nanty Glo to Dilltown
Location: Cambria and Indiana Counties
Length: 15.5 miles (will be 19.5 miles when completed)
Surface: Crushed stone

Contact:
Ed Patterson, Director
Indiana County Parks
RD 2, Box 157-J
Indiana, PA 15701-9802
(412)463-8636

⓰ Great Shamokin Path

Endpoints: Yatesboro to Numine
Location: Armstrong County
Length: 4.0 miles
Surface: Gravel and original ballast

Contact:
Pam Meade, President
Cowanshannock Creek
Watershed Association
P.O. Box 307
Rural Valley, PA 16249-0307
(412)783-6692

⑰ Heart's Content Cross-Country Ski Trail

Endpoints: Allegheny National Forest
Location: Warren County
Length: 3.7 miles of 7.7-mile trail is on abandoned rail corridor
Surface: Grass and dirt

Contact:
Karen Mollander
District Ranger
Allegheny National Forest
Sheffield Ranger District
Route 6
Sheffield, PA 16347
(814)968-3232

⑱ Indian Creek Valley Hiking and Biking Trail

Endpoints: Indian Head to Champion
Location: Fayette County
Length: 5.0 miles
Surface: Original ballast

Contact:
Evelyn Dix, Secretary
Salt Lick Township
Municipal Building
P.O. Box 403
Melcroft, PA 15462-0403
(412)455-2866

⑲ Iron Horse Trail

Endpoints: Big Spring State Park to New Germantown
Location: Perry County
Length: 10.0 miles
Surface: Original ballast and dirt

Contact:
Ernie Geanette
Resource Management Assistant
Bureau of Forestry
RD 1, Box 42A
Blain, PA 17006-9734
(717)536-3191

⑳ Kinzua Bridge Trail

Endpoints: Kinzua Bridge State Park
Location: McKean County
Length: 0.5 miles
Surface: Original ballast

Contact:
Trail Manager
Kinzua Bridge State Park
c/o Bendigo State Park
P.O. Box A
Johnsonburg, PA 15845
(814)965-2646

㉑ Lambs Creek Hike and Bike Trail

Endpoints: Mansfield to Lamb's Creek Recreation Area
Location: Tioga County
Length: 3.2 miles
Surface: Asphalt

Contact:
Richard Koeppel
Park Manager
U.S. Army Corps of Engineers
RD 1, Box 65
Tioga, PA 16946-9733
(717)835-5281

㉒ Lancaster Junction Trail

Endpoints: Lancaster Junction to Landisville
Location: Lancaster County
Length: 2.3 miles
Surface: Dirt and cinder

Contact:
John Gerencser
Recreation Coordinator
Lancaster County Parks & Recreation
1050 Rockford Road
Lancaster, PA 17602-4624
(717)299-8215

㉓ Le Tort Spring Run Nature Trail

Endpoints: Carlisle to South Middleton
Location: Cumberland County
Length: 1.0 mile of 1.4-mile trail is on abandoned rail corridor
Surface: Original ballast and grass

Contact:
Kenwood Giffhorn
Executive Director
Le Tort Regional Authority
415 Franklin Street
Carlisle, PA 17013-1859
(717)245-0508

㉔ Lehigh Gorge State Park Trail

Endpoints: Jim Thorpe to White Haven
Location: Carbon and Luzerne Counties
Length: 26.0 miles
Surface: Crushed stone and original ballast

on certain sections

Contact:
Bob Kerr
Lehigh Gorge State Park
RR 1, Box 81
White Haven, PA 18661
(717)443-0400

㉕ Little Drummer Historic Pathway

Endpoints: Allegheny National Forest
Location: Elk County
Length: 3.5 miles
Surface: Dirt

Contact:
Mary Hosmer
Recreation Specialist
Allegheny National Forest
222 Liberty Street
Warren, PA 16365
(814)723-5150

㉖ Lower Trail

Endpoints: Alexandria to Williamsburg
Location: Blair and Huntingdon Counties
Length: 11.0 miles
Surface: Crushed stone and original ballast

Contact:
Jennifer Barefoot
or Palmer Brown
Rails-to-Trails of Blair County
P.O. Box 592
Hollidaysburg, PA 16648
(814)832-2400

㉗ Lycoming Creek Bikeway

Endpoints: Williamsport to Loyalsock
Location: Lycoming County
Length: 1.5 miles of 3.3-mile trail is on abandoned rail corridor
Surface: Asphalt

Contact:
Mark Murawski
Transportation Planner
Lycoming County Planning
48 West Third Street
Williamsport, PA 17701-6536
(717)327-2230

㉘ Mill Creek Loop Trail

Endpoints: Allegheny National Forest
Location: Elk County
Length: 3.1 miles of 16.7-mile trail is on abandoned rail corridor
Surface: Grass and dirt

Contact:
Leon Blashock
District Ranger
Allegheny National Forest
Ridgway Ranger District
RD 1, Box 28A
Ridgway, PA 15853
(814)776-6172

㉙ Minister Creek Trail

Endpoints: Allegheny National Forest
Location: Forest and Warren Counties
Length: 0.6 miles of 6.6-mile trail is on abandoned rail corridor
Surface: Grass and dirt

Contact:
Karen Mollander
District Ranger
Allegheny National Forest
Sheffield Ranger District
Route 6
Sheffield, PA 16347
(814)968-3232

㉚ Montour Trail

Endpoints: Coraopolis to Clairton
Location: Allegheny and Washington Counties
Length: 20 miles (will be 55 miles when completed)
Surface: Crushed stone

Cecil Section
Contact:
Don Berty
Montour Trail Council
P.O. Box 11866
Pittsburgh, PA 15228-0866
(412)221-6406

Coraopolis to Champion Section
Contact:
Tom Fix
Montour Trail Council
P.O. Box 11866
Pittsburgh, PA 15228-0866
(412)831-2030

㉛ O&W Road Trail

Endpoints: Preston to New York state line
Location: Lackawanna, Susquehanna and Wayne Counties
Length: 6 miles (will be 32 miles when completed)
Surface: Gravel and dirt

Contact:
Phil Pass
Rail Trail Council of Northeast Pennsylvania
P.O. Box 100
Clifford, PA 18413-0100
(717)222-3333

㉜ Oil Creek State Park Trail

Endpoints: Petroleum Centre to Titusville
Location: Crawford and Venango Counties
Length: 8.0 miles of 9.7-mile trail is on abandoned rail corridor
Surface: Asphalt

Contact:
Douglas Finger
Park Manager
Oil Creek State Park
RR 1, Box 207
Oil City, PA 16301
(814)676-5915

㉝ Old Railroad Trail

Endpoints: Big Pocono State Park to Crescent Lake
Location: Monroe County
Length: 8.4 miles
Surface: Original ballast

Contact:
Ronald Dixon, Park Manager
Big Pocono State Park
c/o Tobyhanna State Park
P.O. Box 387
Tobyhanna, PA 18466-0387
(717)894-8336

㉞ Old Salem Trail

Endpoints: Salem to Osgood
Location: Mercer County
Length: 2.5 miles
Surface: Original ballast

Contact:
Sheryl Peterson, President
Mercer County Rails-to-Trails
681 N. Neshannock Road
Hermitage, PA 16148
(412)981-4489

㉟ PW&S Railroad Hiking-Biking Trail

Endpoints: Forbes State Forest
Location: Somerset and Westmoreland Counties
Length: 9.5 miles of 31.0-mile trail is on abandoned rail corridor
Surface: Gravel and dirt

Contact:
Lysle Sherwin
Executive Director
Loyalhanna Watershed Association
P.O. Box 561
Ligonier, PA 15658-0561
(412)238-7560

㊱ Penns Creek Path

Endpoints: Poe Paddy State Park
Location: Centre and Mifflin Counties
Length: 2.9 miles
Surface: Original ballast

Contact:
Thomas Thwaites, President
Mid State Trail Association
P.O. Box 167
Boalsburg, PA 16827-0167
(814)237-7703

㊲ Pine Creek Gorge Trail

Endpoints: Tioga State Forest
Location: Lycoming and Tioga Counties
Length: 62.0 miles
Surface: Original ballast

Contact:
Jack Sherwood
Bureau of Forestry
Department of Environmental Resources
P.O. Box 94
Route 287 South
Wellsboro, PA 16901
(717)724-2868

⓷⓼ Plainfield Township Recreation Trail

Endpoints: Plainfield
Location: Northampton County
Length: 6.7 miles
Surface: Crushed stone and gravel

Contact:
Jenny Koehler, Treasurer
Plainfield Township
517 Getz Road
Nazareth, PA 18064
(610)759-6944

⓷⓽ Pymatuning State Park Trail

Endpoints: Pymatuning State Park
Location: Crawford County
Length: 2.9 miles
Surface: Original ballast

Contact:
Dennis Mihoci
Park Manager
Pymatuning State Park
P.O. Box 425
Jamestown, PA 16134
(412)932-3141

⓸⓪ Railroad Grade Trail

Endpoints: Ives Run Recreation Area
Location: Tioga County
Length: 2.6 miles
Surface: Original ballast

Contact:
Dina Dreisdach
or Richard Koeppel
U.S. Army Corps of Engineers
RD 1, Box 65
Tioga, PA 16946-9733
(717)835-5287

⓸⓵ Roaring Run Trail

Endpoints: Kiskiminetas
Location: Armstrong County
Length: 3.5 miles (will be 5.0 miles when completed)
Surface: Crushed stone

Contact:
Andy Schreffler, Director
Roaring Run Watershed Association
P.O. Box 40
Spring Church, PA 15686
(412)568-1483

⓸⓶ Rocky Gap ATV/Bike Trail

Endpoints: Allegheny National Forest
Location: Warren County
Length: 0.4 miles of 15.5-mile trail is on abandoned rail corridor
Surface: Grass and dirt

Contact:
Karen Mollander
District Ranger
Allegheny National Forest
Sheffield Ranger District
Route 6
Sheffield, PA 16347
(814)968-3232

⓸⓷ Samuel Justus Recreation Trail

Endpoints: Franklin to Oil City
Location: Venango County
Length: 5.8 miles (will be 12.9 miles when completed)
Surface: Asphalt with parallel ballast treadway

Contact:
Richard Castonguay
Secretary
Cranberry Township
P.O. Box 378
Seneca, PA 16346-0378
(814)676-8812

⓸⓸ Schuylkill River Trail

Endpoints: Philadelphia to Valley Forge
Location: Montgomery County
Length: 11.5 miles of 21.0-mile trail is on abandoned rail corridor
Surface: Asphalt

Contact:
John Wood, Chief
Open Space Planning
Montgomery County
Planning Commission
Court House
Norristown, PA 19404
(610)278-3736

⁴⁵ Stony Valley Railroad Grade

Endpoints: Dauphin to Lebanon Reservoir
Location: Dauphin, Lebanon and Schuylkill Counties
Length: 22.0 miles
Surface: Crushed stone

Contact:
Roland Bergner, Chief
Federal-State Coordination Division
Pennsylvania Game Commission
2001 Elmerton Avenue
Harrisburg, PA 17100-9797
(717)787-9612

⁴⁶ Struble Trail

Endpoints: Downingtown
Location: Chester County
Length: 2.5 miles (will be 16 miles when completed)
Surface: Crushed stone

Contact:
Chester County Parks & Recreation Department
601 West Town Road
Suite 160
West Chester, PA 19382
(610)344-6415

⁴⁷ Switchback Railroad Trail

Endpoints: Summit Hill to Jim Thorpe
Location: Carbon County
Length: 18.0 miles
Surface: Original ballast

Contact:
Dennis DeMara
Park Director
Carbon County Park and Recreation Department
625 Lentz Trail Road
Jim Thorpe, PA 18229
(717)325-3669

⁴⁸ Thun Trail

Endpoints: Reading to Stowe
Location: Berks County
Length: 2.5 miles of 15.0-mile trail is on abandoned rail corridor
Surface: Original ballast

Contact:
Victor Yarnell
Managing Director
Schuylkill River Greenways Association
The Old Mill
960 Old Mill Road
Wyomissing, PA 19610
(610)372-3916

⁴⁹ Tidioute Riverside RecTrek Trail

Endpoints: Allegheny National Forest
Location: Warren County
Length: 4.5 miles
Surface: Original ballast

Contact:
Mary Hosmer
Recreation Specialist
Allegheny National Forest
222 Liberty Street
Warren, PA 16365
(814)723-5150

⁵⁰ Towpath Bike Trail

Endpoints: Bethlehem to Palmer
Location: Northampton County
Length: 7.8 miles
Surface: Asphalt

Contact:
H. Robert Daws, Chair
Palmer Township Board of Supervisors
P.O. Box 3039
Palmer, PA 18043-3039
(215)253-7191

⁵¹ Twin Lakes Trail

Endpoints: Allegheny National Forest
Location: Elk and Warren Counties
Length: 1.3 miles of 14.7-mile trail is on abandoned rail corridor
Surface: Grass and dirt

Contact:
Leon Blashock
District Ranger
Allegheny National Forest
Ridgway Ranger District
RD 1, Box 28A
Ridgway, PA 15853
(814)776-6172

52 York County Heritage Rail-Trail

Endpoints: New Freedom to Maryland state line
Location: York County
Length: 1.5 miles (will be 22 miles when completed)
Surface: Crushed stone

Contact:
Catherine Case
Project Coordinator
York County Parks
400 Mundis Race Road
York, PA 17402
(717)771-9440

53 Youghiogheny River Trail–North

Endpoints: Connellsville to McKeesport
Location: Allegheny, Fayette and Westmoreland Counties
Length: 15 miles (will be 43 miles when completed)
Surface: Crushed stone with parallel dirt treadway

Contact:
Robert G. McKinley
Trail Manager
Regional Trail Corporation
101 North Water Street
P.O. Box 95
West Newton, PA 15089
(412)872-5586

54 Youghiogheny River Trail–South

Endpoints: Confluence to Connellsville
Location: Fayette County
Length: 28.0 miles
Surface: Crushed stone

Contact:
Douglas Hoehn
Park Superintendent
Ohiopyle State Park
P.O. Box 105
Ohiopyle, PA 15470-0105
(412)329-8591

RHODE ISLAND

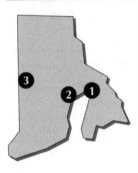

1 East Bay Bicycle Path

Endpoints: Bristol to Providence
Location: Bristol County
Length: 12.0 miles of 14.5-mile trail is on abandoned rail corridor
Surface: Asphalt

Contact:
Kevin O'Malley
Regional Manager
Colt State Park
Bristol, RI 02809
(401)253-7482

2 Phenix–Harris Riverwalk

Endpoints: West Warwick
Location: Kent County
Length: 0.5 miles (will be 1.2 miles when completed)
Surface: Dirt

Contact:
Bill Cocroft, Chairman
Pawtuxet River Authority
P.O. Box 336
West Warwick, RI 02893
(401)828-5650

3 Trestle Trail

Endpoints: Coventry Center to Connecticut state line
Location: Kent County
Length: 8.0 miles
Surface: Gravel, original ballast and dirt

Contact:
Ginny Leslie
Senior Planner
Rhode Island Department of Environmental Management
Division of Planning and Development
83 Park Street
Providence, RI 02903
(401)277-2776 ext. 4309

SOUTH CAROLINA

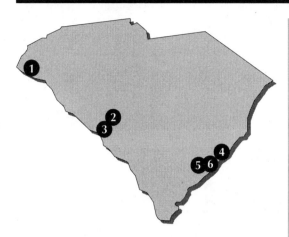

❶ Blue Ridge Railroad Historical Trail

Endpoints: Stumphouse Tunnel to Walhalla
Location: Oconee County
Length: 5.0 miles
Surface: Wood chips and dirt

Contact:
Hurley Badders
Executive Director
Pendleton Historic and
Recreational Commission
P.O. Box 565
Pendleton, SC 29670-0565
(803)646-3782

❷ Cathedral Aisle Trail

Endpoints: Aiken
Location: Aiken County
Length: 1.0 mile
Surface: Dirt

Contact:
Dr. Harry Shealy, Trustee
Hitchcock Foundation
P.O. Box 1702
Aiken, SC 29802-1702
(803)648-2040

❸ North Augusta Trail

Endpoints: North Augusta
Location: Aiken County
Length: 3.2 miles (will be 5.2 miles when completed)
Surface: Asphalt and gravel

Contact:
J. Robert Brooks, Director
Parks & Recreation
Department
P.O. Box 6400
North Augusta, SC 29841
(803)441-4300

❹ Swamp Fox National Recreation Trail

Endpoints: Francis Marion National Forest
Location: Berkeley and Charleston Counties
Length: 6.0 miles of 15.0-mile trail is on abandoned rail corridor
Surface: Original ballast

Contact:
Sharon Rhodes
Recreation Forester
Francis Marion National
Forest
P.O. Box 788
McClellanville, SC 29458
(803)887-3257

❺ West Ashley Bikeway

Endpoints: Charleston
Location: Charleston County
Length: 2.0 miles (will be 2.7 miles when completed)
Surface: Asphalt

Contact:
Kirk West
Landscape Architect
Charleston Department
of Parks
823 Meeting Street
Charleston, SC 29403
(803)724-7321

❻ West Ashley Greenway

Endpoints: Charleston
Location: Charleston County
Length: 7.5 miles
Surface: Crushed stone, grass and dirt

Contact:
Kirk West
Landscape Architect
Charleston Dept. of Parks
823 Meeting Street
Charleston, SC 29403
(803)724-7321

SOUTH DAKOTA

❶ George S. Mickelson Trail

Endpoints: Deadwood to Edgemont
Location: Custer, Fall River, Lawrence and Pennington Counties
Length: 47 miles (will be 109.5 miles when completed)
Surface: Crushed stone and gravel

Contact:
Kim Raap
South Dakota Game, Fish, and Parks Department
523 East Capitol Avenue
Pierre, SD 57501-3182
(605)773-4230

❶ Bald River Trail

Endpoints: Cherokee National Forest
Location: Monroe County
Length: 5.6 miles
Surface: Dirt

Contact:
Larry Fleming
District Ranger
Cherokee National Forest
Tellico Ranger District
250 Ranger Station Road
Tellico Plains, TN 37385
(615)253-2520

❷ Conasauga River Trail

Endpoints: Cherokee National Forest
Location: Monroe County
Length: 2.5 miles of 4.5-mile trail is on abandoned rail corridor
Surface: Dirt

Contact:
Larry Fleming
District Ranger
Cherokee National Forest
Tellico Ranger District
250 Ranger Station Road
Tellico Plains, TN 37385
(615)253-2520

❸ Crowder Branch Trail

Endpoints: Cherokee National Forest
Location: Monroe County
Length: 1.5 miles of 2.6-mile trail is on abandoned rail corridor
Surface: Dirt

Contact:
Larry Fleming
District Ranger
Cherokee National Forest
Tellico Ranger District
250 Ranger Station Road
Tellico Plains, TN 37385
(615)253-2520

❹ Grassy Branch Trail

Endpoints: Cherokee National Forest
Location: Monroe County
Length: 2.7 miles of 3.2-mile trail is on abandoned rail corridor
Surface: Dirt

Contact:
Larry Fleming
District Ranger
Cherokee National Forest
Tellico Ranger District
250 Ranger Station Road
Tellico Plains, TN 37385
(615)253-2520

❺ Hemlock Trail

Endpoints: Cherokee National Forest
Location: Monroe County
Length: 2.0 miles of 3.0-mile trail is on abandoned rail corridor
Surface: Dirt

Contact:
Larry Fleming
District Ranger
Cherokee National Forest
Tellico Ranger District
250 Ranger Station Road
Tellico Plains, TN 37385
(615)253-2520

❻ Laurel Branch Trail

Endpoints: Cherokee National Forest
Location: Monroe County
Length: 2.0 miles of 3.0-mile trail is on abandoned rail corridor
Surface: Dirt

Contact:
Larry Fleming
District Ranger
Cherokee National Forest
Tellico Ranger District
250 Ranger Station Road
Tellico Plains, TN 37385
(615)253-2520

❼ Long Branch Trail

Endpoints: Cherokee National Forest
Location: Monroe County
Length: 1.5 miles of 2.7-mile trail is on abandoned rail corridor
Surface: Dirt

Contact:
Larry Fleming
District Ranger
Cherokee National Forest
Tellico Ranger District
250 Ranger Station Road
Tellico Plains, TN 37385
(615)253-2520

❽ McNabb Creek Trail

Endpoints: Cherokee National Forest
Location: Monroe County
Length: 2.0 miles of 3.9-mile trail is on abandoned rail corridor
Surface: Original ballast

Contact:
Larry Fleming
District Ranger
Cherokee National Forest
Tellico Ranger District
250 Ranger Station Road
Tellico Plains, TN 37385
(615)253-2520

❾ North Fork Citico Trail

Endpoints: Cherokee National Forest
Location: Monroe County
Length: 5.0 miles
Surface: Original ballast

Contact:
Larry Fleming
District Ranger
Cherokee National Forest
Tellico Ranger District
250 Ranger Station Road
Tellico Plains, TN 37385
(615)253-2520

❿ South Fork Citico Trail

Endpoints: Cherokee National Forest
Location: Monroe County
Length: 7.0 miles of 8.1-mile trail is on abandoned rail corridor
Surface: Dirt

Contact:
Larry Fleming
District Ranger
Cherokee National Forest
Tellico Ranger District
250 Ranger Station Road
Tellico Plains, TN 37385
(615)253-2520

Texas

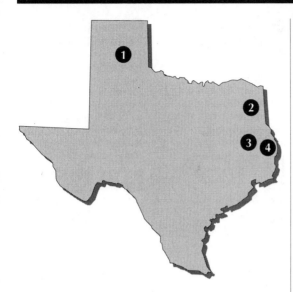

❸ Four-C Hiking Trail

Endpoints: Davy Crockett National Forest
Location: Houston County
Length: 16.0 miles of 20.0-mile trail is on abandoned rail corridor
Surface: Original ballast and dirt

Contact:
Duane Strock
Landscape Architect
Davy Crockett National Forest
701 North 1st Street
Lufkin, TX 75901-3057
(409)639-8529

❶ Caprock Canyons State Park Trailway

Endpoints: Estelline to South Plains
Location: Briscoe, Floyd and Hall Counties
Length: 24.0 miles (will be 64.2 miles when completed)
Surface: Original ballast

Contact:
Russell Sargent
Maintenance & Operations Specialist
Texas Parks and Wildlife Department
302 North Willis Street
Suite 15
Abilene, TX 79603
(915)676-2241

❷ Cargill Long Park Trail

Endpoints: Longview
Location: Gregg County
Length: 2.5 miles (will be 3.0 miles when completed)
Surface: Asphalt

Contact:
Paul Boorman, Manager
Longview Parks and Leisure Services
P.O. Box 1952
Longview, TX 75606-1952
(903)757-4555

❹ Sawmill Hiking Trail

Endpoints: Angelina National Forest
Location: Angelina and Jasper Counties
Length: 4.5 miles of 5.5-mile trail is on abandoned rail corridor
Surface: Dirt

Contact:
Catherine Albers
Resource Forester
Angelina National Forest
Angelina Ranger District
1907 Atkinson Drive
Lufkin, TX 75901-2505
(409)639-8620

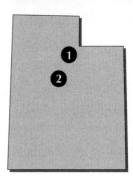

❶ Historic Union Pacific Rail Trail

Endpoints: Echo Junction to Park City
Location: Summit County
Length: 28.0 miles (will be 30.5 miles when completed)
Surface: Asphalt and crushed stone

Contact:
Larry Stump, Park Manager
Utah Department of
Natural Resources
Division of Parks &
Recreation
P.O. Box 309
Heber City, UT 84032
(801)649-3602

❷ Provo Jordan River Parkway Trail

Endpoints: Provo to Provo Canyon
Location: Utah County
Length: 15.0 miles of 43.0-mile trail is on abandoned rail corridor
Surface: Asphalt with parallel dirt treadway

Contact:
Clyde Naylor, Engineer
Utah County
2855 South State
Provo, UT 84606
(801)370-8600

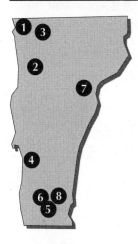

❶ Alburg Recreational Rail-Trail

Endpoints: East Alburg to Alburg
Location: Grand Isle County
Length: 7.0 miles
Surface: Original ballast

Contact:
Charles Vile
State Lands Wildlife Forester
Vermont Department of Forests, Parks & Recreation
111 West Street
Essex Junction, VT 05452
(802)879-6565

❷ Burlington Waterfront Bikeway

Endpoints: Burlington
Location: Chittendon County
Length: 8.5 miles
Surface: Asphalt

Contact:
Robert Whalen
Superintendent
Burlington Department of Parks & Recreation
1 LaValley Lane
Burlington, VT 05401-2779
(802)865-7247

❸ Central Vermont Rail Trail

Endpoints: St. Albans to Richford
Location: Franklin County
Length: 27.0 miles
Surface: Original ballast

Contact:
Charles Vile
State Lands Wildlife Forester
Vermont Department of Forests, Parks & Recreation
111 West Street
Essex Junction, VT 05452
(802)879-6565

❹ Delaware and Hudson Rail-Trail

Endpoints: West Rupert to Castleton
Location: Bennington and Rutland Counties
Length: 19.8 miles
Surface: Original ballast

Contact:
Trails Coordinator
Department of Forests, Parks & Recreation
Vermont Agency of Natural Resources
RR 2, Box 261
Pittsford, VT 05763
(802)483-2314

❺ East Branch Trail

Endpoints: Green Mountain National Forest
Location: Windham County
Length: 4.5 miles of 5.1-mile trail is on abandoned rail corridor
Surface: Gravel

Contact:
Robert Pramuk
Recreation Forester
Green Mountain National Forest
231 North Main Street
Rutland, VT 05701
(802)747-6700

❻ Lye Brook Trail

Endpoints: Green
Mountain National Forest
Location: Bennington and
Windham Counties
Length: 4.1 miles of 9.7-
mile trail is on abandoned
rail corridor
Surface: Gravel

Contact:
Robert Pramuk
Recreation Forester
Green Mountain National
Forest
231 North Main Street
Rutland, VT 05701
(802)747-6700

❼ Montpelier and Wells River Trail

Endpoints: Groton State
Forest
Location: Caledonia
County
Length: 17.0 miles
Surface: Gravel and
original ballast

Contact:
David Willard
Trails Coordinator
Vermont Agency of Natural
Resources
Department of Forests,
Parks & Recreation
184 Portland Street
St. Johnsbury, VT 05819
(802)748-8787

❽ Railroad Bed Trail

Endpoints: Jamaica State
Park
Location: Windham
County
Length: 3.0 miles
Surface: Gravel and
original ballast

Contact:
David Willard
Trails Coordinator
Vermont Agency of Natural
Resources
Department of Forests,
Parks & Recreation
184 Portland Street
St. Johnbury, VT 05819
(802)748-8787

VIRGINIA

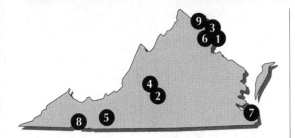

❶ Accotink Trail

Endpoints: Springfield
Location: Fairfax County
Length: 2.2 miles of 3.8-mile trail is on abandoned rail corridor
Surface: Gravel

Contact:
Lake Accotink Park
3701 Pender Drive
Fairfax, VA 22030
(703)569-0285

❷ Blackwater Creek Natural Area Bikeway

Endpoints: Lynchburg
Location: Amherst and Campbell Counties
Length: 4 miles (will be 10 miles when completed)
Surface: Asphalt and gravel

Contact:
Michael Hayslett, Naturalist
City of Lynchburg Parks & Recreation Department
301 Grove Street
Lynchburg, VA 24501
(804)847-1640

❸ Bluemont Junction Trail

Endpoints: Bluemont Park to Ballston
Location: Arlington County
Length: 1.3 miles
Surface: Asphalt

Contact:
Ritch Viola
Arlington County
Department of Public Works
2100 Clarendon Boulevard
Suite 717
Arlington, VA 22201-5445
(703)358-3699

❹ Chessie Nature Trail

Endpoints: Lexington to Buena Vista
Location: Rockbridge County
Length: 7.5 miles
Surface: Crushed stone

Contact:
Louise Dooley
Assistant Vice President
VMI Foundation
P.O. Box 932
Lexington, VA 24450-0932
(703)464-7221

❺ New River Trail State Park

Endpoints: Pulaski to Galax with spur to Fries
Location: Carroll, Grayson, Pulaski and Wythe Counties
Length: 55 miles (will be 57 miles when completed)
Surface: Cinder

Contact:
Mark Hufeisen
or Doug Smith
Park Manager
New River Trail State Park
Route 1, Box 81-X
Austinville, VA 24312
(540)699-6778

❻ Orange and Alexandria Historical Trail

Endpoints: Lake Accotink Park
Location: Fairfax County
Length: 3.0 miles
Surface: Crushed stone

Contact:
Lake Accotink Park
3701 Pender Drive
Fairfax, VA 22030
(703)569-0285

❼ Park Connector Bikeway

Endpoints: Mt. Trashmore to Princess Anne Park
Location: Virginia Beach County
Length: 2.7 miles of 4.9-mile trail is on abandoned rail corridor
Surface: Asphalt

Contact:
Travis Campbell
Department of Planning
Room 115, Operations
Building
2405 Courthouse Road
Virginia Beach, VA 23456
(804)427-4621

❽ Virginia Creeper National Recreation Trail

Endpoints: Abingdon to White Top
Location: Grayson and Washington Counties
Length: 34.1 miles
Surface: Gravel and dirt

Abingdon to Damascus Section

Contact:
Abingdon Convention and Visitors Bureau
335 Cummings Street
Abingdon, VA 24210
(703)676-2282

Damascus to White Top Section

Contact:
Area Ranger
Mt. Rogers National Recreation Area
Route 1, Box 303
Marion, VA 24354-9700
(703)783-5196

❾ Washington and Old Dominion Railroad Regional Park

Endpoints: Arlington to Purcellville
Location: Arlington, Fairfax and Loudoun Counties
Length: 45.0 miles
Surface: Asphalt with parallel crushed stone treadway

Contact:
Paul McCray, Park Manager
Northern Virginia Regional Park Authority
5400 Ox Road
Fairfax Station, VA 22039
(703)729-0596

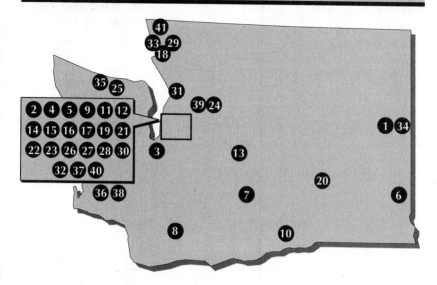

❶ Benn Burr Trail

Endpoints: Spokane
Location: Spokane County
Length: 1.1 miles
Surface: Gravel and dirt

Contact:
Taylor Bressler
Division Manager
City of Spokane Parks Dept.
N. 809 Washington Street
Spokane, WA 99201-2233
(509)625-6655

❷ Burke-Gilman Trail

Endpoints: Seattle to
Bothell
Location: King County
Length: 18.0 miles
Surface: Asphalt

Contacts:
Bicycle/Pedestrian
Coordinator
Seattle Engineering Dept.
708 Municipal Building
600 Fourth Avenue
Seattle, WA 98104
(206)684-7583

Tom Eksten
Trails Coordinator
King County Office of
Open Space
708 Smith Tower
506 Second Avenue
Seattle, WA 98104
(206)296-7800

❸ Chehalis Western Trail

Endpoints: Woodard Bay
National Resource
Conservation Area
Location: Thurston County
Length: 6.0 miles
Surface: Asphalt

Contact:
Bud Clark, District Manager
Washington Department
of Natural Resources
1405 Rush Road
Chehalis, WA 98532-8727
(206)748-2383

❹ City of Snoqualmie Centennial Trail

Endpoints: Snoqualmie
Location: King County
Length: 0.5 miles
Surface: Asphalt

Contact:
Leroy Gmazel, Director
Community Development
City of Snoqualmie
P.O. Box 987
Snoqualmie, WA 98065
(206)888-5337

115

❺ Coal Creek Park Trail

Endpoints: Coal Creek Park
Location: King County
Length: 1.0 mile
Surface: Original ballast and dirt

Contact:
Tom Eksten
Trails Coordinator
King County Office of Open Space
708 Smith Tower
506 Second Avenue
Seattle, WA 98104
(206)296-7800

❻ Colfax Trail

Endpoints: Colfax
Location: Whitman County
Length: 3.0 miles
Surface: Dirt

Contact:
Brian Carroll, Supervisor
Recreation & Operations
Whitman County Parks and Recreation
310 North Main
Colfax, WA 99111
(509)397-6238

❼ Cowiche Canyon Trail

Endpoints: Yakima
Location: Yakima County
Length: 2.9 miles
Surface: Gravel and dirt

Contact:
David Hagan, President
Cowiche Canyon Conservancy
P.O. Box 877
Yakima, WA 98907
(509)966-3880

❽ Dry Creek Trail

Endpoints: Gifford Pinchot National Forest
Location: Skamania County
Length: 1.5 miles of 4.0-mile trail is on abandoned rail corridor
Surface: Original ballast

Contact:
Dorris Tai
Trails Coordinator
Gifford Pinchot National Forest
6926 East Fourth Plain Blvd.
P.O. Box 8944
Vancouver, WA 98668-8944
(360)750-5011

❾ Duwamish Bikeway

Endpoints: Seattle
Location: King County
Length: 2.0 miles of 4.5-mile trail is on abandoned rail corridor
Surface: Asphalt

Contact:
Bicycle/Pedestrian Coordinator
Seattle Engineering Department
708 Municipal Building
600 Fourth Avenue
Seattle, WA 98104-1826
(206)684-7583

❿ Grandview— Sunnyside Pathway

Endpoints: Grandview
Location: Yakima County
Length: 1.0 mile of 6.3-mile trail is on abandoned rail corridor
Surface: Asphalt

Contact:
David Veley
Assistant Director
Yakima County Parks
1000 Ahtanum Road
Union Grove, WA 98903
(509)575-4151

⓫ Green to Cedar River Trail

Endpoints: Maple Valley to Lake Wilderness
Location: King County
Length: 4.0 miles (will be 8.0 miles when completed)
Surface: Original ballast

Contact:
Tom Eksten
Trails Coordinator
King County Office of Open Space
708 Smith Tower
506 Second Avenue
Seattle, WA 98104
(206)296-7800

⑫ Iron Goat Trail

Endpoints: Mt. Baker
Snoqualmie National Forest
Location: King County
Length: 3.6 miles of 4.0-
mile trail is on abandoned
rail corridor
Surface: Crushed stone
and original ballast

Contact:
Ian Ritchie, Archaeologist
Mt. Baker Snoqualmie
National Forest
Skykomish Ranger District
P.O. Box 305
Skykomish, WA 98288-0305
(206)677-2412

⑬ Iron Horse State Park

Endpoints: North Bend to
Vantage
Location: King and
Kittitas Counties
Length: 82 miles (will be
113 miles when completed)
Surface: Gravel and
original ballast

Contact:
Colleen McKee, Park Ranger
Iron Horse State Park
P.O. Box 26
Easton, WA 98925
(509)656-2586

⑭ Issaquah Creek Trail

Endpoints: High Point to
Issaquah
Location: King County
Length: 2.0 miles
Surface: Original ballast

Contact:
Tom Eksten
Trails Coordinator
King County Office of
Open Space
708 Smith Tower
506 Second Avenue
Seattle, WA 98104
(206)296-7800

⑮ Issaquah Trail

Endpoints: Issaquah
Location: King County
Length: 2.0 miles
Surface: Concrete

Contact:
Margaret McCleod
Issaquah Parks &
Recreation Department
P.O. Box 1307
Issaquah, WA 98027
(206)313-0650

⑯ Iverson Railroad Grade Trail

Endpoints: Tiger
Mountain State Park
Location: King County
Length: 2.0 miles
Surface: Dirt

Contact:
Jim Matthews
Recreation Forester
Tiger Mountain State Forest
P.O. Box 68
Enumclaw, WA 98022
(206)825-1631

⑰ King County Interurban Trail

Endpoints: Tuckwila to
Pacific
Location: King County
Length: 15 miles (will be
16 miles when completed)
Surface: Asphalt

Contact:
Tom Eksten
Trails Coordinator
King County Office of
Open Space
708 Smith Tower
506 Second Avenue
Seattle, WA 98104
(206)296-7800

⑱ Lower Padden Creek Trail

Endpoints: Bellingham
Location: Whatcom
County
Length: 0.8 miles
Surface: Crushed stone

Contact:
Leslie Bryson, Manager
Design & Development
Bellingham Parks &
Recreation Department
210 Lottie Street
Bellingham, WA 98225
(360)676-6985

⓳ Middle Fork Snoqualmie River Trail

Endpoints: Mt. Baker-Snoqualmie National Forest
Location: King County
Length: 5.0 miles of 17.0-mile trail is on abandoned rail corridor
Surface: Original ballast

Contact:
Thomas Quincy
Forestry Technician
Mt. Baker Snoqualmie National Forest
North Bend Ranger District
42404 S.E. North Bend Way
North Bend, WA 98045
(206)888-1421

⓴ Milwaukee Road Corridor

Endpoints: Iron Horse State Park to Tekoa
Location: Adams, Grant, Spokane and Whitman Counties
Length: 145.0 miles
Surface: Crushed stone, original ballast and dirt

Contact:
James Munroe
Special Land Manager
SE Region
Washington Department of Natural Resources
2211 Airport Road
Ellensburg, WA 98926
(509)925-6131

㉑ Myrtle Edwards Park Trail

Endpoints: Seattle
Location: King County
Length: 1.2 miles of 2.5-mile trail is on abandoned rail corridor
Surface: Asphalt with parallel dirt treadway

Contact:
Bicycle/Pedestrian Coordinator
Seattle Engineering Dept.
708 Municipal Building
600 Fourth Avenue
Seattle, WA 98104
(206)684-7583

㉒ Necklace Valley Trail

Endpoints: Skykomish
Location: King County
Length: 1.2 miles of 8.0-mile trail is on abandoned rail corridor
Surface: Dirt

Contact:
Tom Davis, Trail Specialist
Skykomish Ranger District
P.O. Box 305
Skykomish, WA 98288
(206)677-3260

㉓ Northwest Timber Trail

Endpoints: Tiger Mountain State Forest
Location: King County
Length: 2.2 miles
Surface: Gravel and dirt

Contact:
Jim Matthews
Recreation Forester
Tiger Mountain State Forest
P.O. Box 68
Enumclaw, WA 98022
(206)825-1631

㉔ Pacific Crest National Scenic Trail

Endpoints: Stevens Pass to Yodelin
Location: Chelan County
Length: 1.5 miles of 36.0-mile trail is on abandoned rail corridor
Surface: Dirt

Contact:
Roger Ross
Trails/Wilderness Coordinator
U.S. Forest Service
Lake Wanache Ranger District
22976 Highway 207
Leavenworth, WA 98826
(509)763-3103

㉕ Port Angeles Waterfront Trail

Endpoints: Port Angeles
Location: Clallam County
Length: 5.0 miles (will be 10 miles when completed)
Surface: Asphalt

Contact:
Scott Brodhun, Director
City of Port Angeles Parks & Recreation
321 East Fifth Street
Port Angeles, WA 98362
(206)457-0411

㉖ Pratt River Trail

Endpoints: Mt. Baker-Snoqualmie National Forest
Location: King County
Length: 6.5 miles of 7.5-mile trail is on abandoned rail corridor
Surface: Original ballast

Contact:
Tom Quincy
Forestry Technician
Mt. Baker-Snoqualmie National Forest
North Bend Ranger District
42404 S.E. North Bend Way
North Bend, WA 98045
(206)888-1421

㉗ Preston Railroad Trail

Endpoints: Tiger Mountain State Forest
Location: King County
Length: 2.7 miles of 5.0-mile trail is on abandoned rail corridor
Surface: Gravel and dirt

Contact:
Jim Matthews
Recreation Forester
Tiger Mountain State Forest
P.O. Box 68
Enumclaw, WA 98022
(206)825-1631

㉘ Preston – Snoqualmie Trail

Endpoints: Preston to Snoqualmie
Location: King County
Length: 6.5 miles (will be 8.5 miles when completed)
Surface: Asphalt

Contact:
Tom Eksten
Trails Coordinator
King County Office of Open Space
708 Smith Tower
506 Second Avenue
Seattle, WA 98104
(206)296-7800

㉙ Railroad Trail

Endpoints: Bellingham
Location: Whatcom County
Length: 2.0 miles of 6.5-mile trail is on abandoned rail corridor
Surface: Crushed stone

 on certain sections

Contact:
Leslie Bryson, Manager
Design & Development
Bellingham Parks and Recreation Department
210 Lottie Street
Bellingham, WA 98225
(360)676-6985

㉚ Seattle Waterfront Pathway

Endpoints: Seattle
Location: King County
Length: 0.8 miles
Surface: Asphalt

Contact:
Bicycle/Pedestrian Coordinator
Seattle Engineering Dept.
708 Municipal Building
600 Fourth Avenue
Seattle, WA 98104
(206)684-7583

㉛ Snohomish County Centennial Trail

Endpoints: Arlington to King County line
Location: Snohomish County
Length: 17.3 miles (will be 44 miles when completed)
Surface: Asphalt with parallel gravel treadway

Contact:
Snohomish County Parks & Recreation Department
3000 Rockefeller Avenue
MS 303
Everett, WA 98201
(206)339-1208

32 Snoqualmie Valley Trail

Endpoints: Carnation to Fall City
Location: King County
Length: 13 miles (will be 18 miles when completed)
Surface: Original ballast

 on certain sections

Contact:
Tom Eksten
Trails Coordinator
King County Office of Open Space
708 Smith Tower
506 Second Avenue
Seattle, WA 98104
(206)296-7800

33 South Bay Trail

Endpoints: Bellingham
Location: Whatcom County
Length: 1.5 miles of 4.4-mile trail is on abandoned rail corridor
Surface: Crushed stone

Contact:
Leslie Bryson, Manager
Design & Development
Bellingham Parks and Recreation Department
210 Lottie Street
Bellingham, WA 98225
(360)676-6985

34 Spokane River Centennial Trail

Endpoints: Spokane to Idaho state line
Location: Spokane County
Length: 10.0 miles of 37.0-mile trail is on abandoned rail corridor
Surface: Asphalt

Contact:
Friends of the Centennial Trail
P.O. Box 351
Spokane, WA 99201
(509)324-1756

35 Spruce Railroad Trail

Endpoints: Olympic National Park
Location: Clallam County
Length: 4.0 miles
Surface: Gravel and dirt

Contact:
Sharon Wray
Supervisor, Visitor Center
Olympic National Park
600 East Park Avenue
Port Angeles, WA 98362
(206)452-0330

36 Sylvia Creek Forestry Trail

Endpoints: Lake Sylvia State Park
Location: Grays Harbor County
Length: 0.5 miles of 2.3-mile trail is on abandoned rail corridor
Surface: Dirt

Contact:
Dan Kincaid, Park Manager
Lake Sylvia State Park
P.O. Box 701
Montesano, WA 98563
(360)249-3621

37 Terminal 91 Bike Path

Endpoints: Seattle
Location: King County
Length: 0.5 miles of 1.0-mile trail is on abandoned rail corridor
Surface: Asphalt

Contact:
Chris Lopez
Property Manager
Port of Seattle
P.O. Box 1209
Seattle, WA 98111-1209
(206)728-3000

㉟ Two Mile Trail

Endpoints: Lake Sylvia State Park
Location: Grays Harbor County
Length: 0.7 miles of 2.3-mile trail is on abandoned rail corridor
Surface: Gravel

 on certain sections

Contact:
Dan Kincaid, Park Manager
Lake Sylvia State Park
P.O. Box 701
Montesano, WA 98563
(360)249-3621

㊴ Wallace Falls Railway Trail

Endpoints: Wallace Falls State Park
Location: Snohomish County
Length: 2.5 miles
Surface: Grass and dirt

Contact:
Susan Evans, Park Ranger
Washington State Parks and Recreation Commission
P.O. Box 230
Gold Bar, WA 98251
(360)793-0420

㊵ West Tiger Railroad Grade

Endpoints: West Tiger State Forest
Location: King County
Length: 4.0 miles
Surface: Original ballast and dirt

Contact:
Jim Matthews
Recreation Forester
Tiger Mountain State Forest
P.O. Box 68
Enumclaw, WA 98022
(206)825-1631

㊶ Whatcom County and Bellingham Interurban Trail

Endpoints: Bellingham to Larrabee State Park
Location: Whatcom County
Length: 5.6 miles
Surface: Crushed stone

Contact:
Roger DeSpain, Director
Whatcom County Parks and Recreation Board
3373 Mount Baker Highway
Bellingham, WA 98226-7500
(206)733-2900

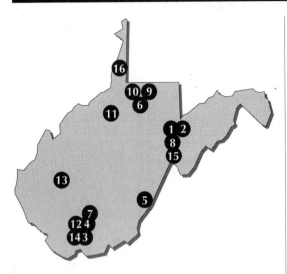

❹ Glade Creek Trail

Endpoints: New River Gorge National River
Location: Raleigh County
Length: 5.6 miles
Surface: Gravel and dirt

Contact:
Joe Kennedy
Superintendent
New River Gorge
National River
P.O. Box 246
Glen Jean, WV 25846
(304)465-0508

❶ Blackwater Canyon Trail

Endpoints: Monongahela National Forest
Location: Tucker County
Length: 12.0 miles
Surface: Gravel and dirt

Contact:
Carol Rucker
Assistant Ranger
Cheat Ranger District
Monongahela National Forest
P.O. Box 368
Parsons, WV 26287
(304)478-3251

❷ Davis Trail

Endpoints: Monongahela National Forest
Location: Tucker County
Length: 2.3 miles
Surface: Dirt

Contact:
Carol Rucker
Assistant Ranger
Cheat Ranger District
Monongahela National Forest
P.O. Box 368
Parsons, WV 26287
(304)478-3251

❸ Dunloup Creek Trail

Endpoints: New River Gorge National River
Location: Fayette County
Length: 1.0 mile
Surface: Gravel and dirt

Contact:
Joe Kennedy
Superintendent
New River Gorge
National River
P.O. Box 246
Glen Jean, WV 25846
(304)465-0508

❺ Greenbrier River Trail

Endpoints: North Caldwell to Cass
Location: Greenbrier and Pocahontas Counties
Length: 75.0 miles
Surface: Gravel and original ballast

 on certain sections

Contacts:
Danny Talbot
Assistant Superintendent
Watoga State Park
Highway 219
Marlinton, WV 24954
(304)799-4087

Gil Willis, President
Greenbrier River Trail
Association
Highway 219
Slaty Fork, WV 26291
(304)572-3771

❻ Harrison County Parks & Recreation Bike and Hike Trail

Endpoints: Clarksburg to Spelter
Location: Harrison County
Length: 6.9 miles
Surface: Cinder

Contact:
Michael Book, Director
Harrison County Parks &
Recreation Commission
301 West Main Street
Clarksburg, WV 26301-2980
(304)624-8619

❼ Kaymoor Trail

Endpoints: New River Gorge National River
Location: Fayette County
Length: 1.8 miles
Surface: Gravel and dirt

Contact:
Joe Kennedy
Superintendent
New River Gorge
National River
P.O. Box 246
Glen Jean, WV 25846
(304)465-0508

❽ Limerock Trail

Endpoints: Monongahela National Forest
Location: Tucker County
Length: 4.1 miles
Surface: Dirt

Contact:
Carol Rucker
Assistant Ranger
Cheat Ranger District
Monongahela National
Forest
P.O. Box 368
Parsons, WV 26287
(304)478-3251

❾ Marion County Trail

Endpoints: Prikets Fort State Park to Fairmont
Location: Marion County
Length: 2.0 miles
Surface: Gravel and cinder

Contact:
Ralph LaRue, Director
Marion County Parks and
Recreation Commission
P.O. Box 1258
Fairmont, WV 26554
(304)363-7037

❿ Narrow Gauge Trail

Endpoints: Babcock State Park
Location: Fayette County
Length: 2.5 miles
Surface: Crushed stone and dirt

Contact:
Mark Wylie, Superintendent
Babcock State Park
HC-35, Box 150
Clifftop, WV 25831
(304)438-3004

⓫ North Bend State Park Rail-Trail

Endpoints: Walker to Wilsonburg
Location: Doddridge, Harrison, Ritchie and Wood Counties
Length: 61 miles
Surface: Crushed stone and gravel

Contact:
Donnie Oates
Superintendent
North Bend State Park
Route 1, Box 221
Cairo, WV 26337
(304)643-2931

⓬ Southside Junction to Brooklyn Trail

Endpoints: New River Gorge National River
Location: Fayette County
Length: 6.4 miles
Surface: Gravel and dirt

Contact:
Joe Kennedy
Superintendent
New River Gorge
National River
P.O. Box 246
Glen Jean, WV 25846
(304)465-0508

⓭ The Elk River Trail

Endpoints: Coonskin Park
Location: Kanawha
County
Length: 1.0 mile
Surface: Gravel

Contact:
Tom Raker, Director
Kanawha County Parks and
Recreation Commission
2000 Coonskin Drive
Charleston, WV 25311-1087
(304)341-8000

⓮ Thurmond to Minden Trail

Endpoints: New River
Gorge National River
Location: Fayette County
Length: 3.2 miles
Surface: Gravel and dirt

Contact:
Joe Kennedy
Superintendent
New River Gorge
National River
P.O. Box 246
Glen Jean, WV 25846
(304)465-0508

⓯ West Fork Trail

Endpoints: Cheat Junction
to Glady
Location: Pocahontas
County
Length: 22.0 miles
Surface: Gravel and
original ballast

Contact:
Gary Willison
Acting Ranger
Monongahela National
Forest
Greenbrier Ranger District
P.O. Box 67
Bartow, WV 24920
(304)456-3335

⓰ Wheeling Heritage Bike & Jogging Trail

Endpoints: Wheeling
Location: Ohio County
Length: 8 miles open in
two separate sections (will
be 16 miles when
completed)

Contact:
Paul McIntire, Director
Department of Development
City-County Building
1500 Chapline Street
Wheeling, WV 26003
(304)234-3701

East to West Section

Endpoints: Wheeling
Length: 1.0 mile (will be
6.0 miles when completed)
Surface: Asphalt

North to South Section

Endpoints: Wheeling
Length: 7 miles (will be 10
miles when completed)
Surface: Asphalt

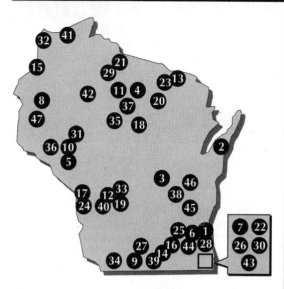

❸ Bannerman Trail

Endpoints: Red Granite to 5 miles south of Wautoma
Location: Waushara County
Length: 7.0 miles
Surface: Grass and dirt

Contact:
Scott Schuman
Parks Superintendent
Waushara County Parks
Wautoma, WI 54982
(414)787-7037

❹ Bearskin State Park Trail

Endpoints: Minocqua to Heafford Junction
Location: Oneida County
Length: 18.4 miles (will be 24.4 miles when completed)
Surface: Crushed stone

Contact:
William Eldred
Trail Manager
Bearskin State Park Trail
4125 Highway M
Boulder Junction, WI 54512
(715)385-2727

❶ 76 Bike Tour

Endpoints: Milwaukee
Location: Milwaukee County
Length: 3.9 miles of 96.4-mile trail is on abandoned rail corridor
Surface: Asphalt

Contact:
Bill Waldron
Planning Analyst
Milwaukee County Parks
9480 Watertown Plank Road
Wauwatosa, WI 53226
(414)257-6100

❷ Ahnapee State Park Trail

Endpoints: Sturgeon Bay to Algoma
Location: Door and Kewaunee Counties
Length: 15.3 miles (will be 18.3 miles when completed)
Surface: Crushed stone

 on certain sections

Contact:
Arnie Lindauer
Ahnapee State Park Trail
c/o Potawatomi State Park
3740 Park Drive
Sturgeon Bay, WI 54235
(414)746-2890

❺ Buffalo River State Park Trail

Endpoints: Fairchild to Mondovi
Location: Buffalo, Eau Claire, Jackson and Trempealeau Counties
Length: 36.4 miles
Surface: Original ballast and dirt

Contact:
Jean Rygiel
Trails Coordinator
Wisconsin Department of Natural Resources
Western Division
1300 West Clairmont Avenue
P.O. Box 4001
Eau Claire, WI 54701-6127
(715)839-1607

❻ Bugline Trail

Endpoints: Menomonee Falls to Merton
Location: Waukesha County
Length: 12.0 miles of 13.0-mile trail is on abandoned rail corridor
Surface: Crushed stone with parallel dirt treadway

 on certain sections

Contact:
David Burch
Senior Landscape Architect
Waukesha County Parks and Planning Commission
1320 Pewaukee Road
Waukesha, WI 53188
(414)548-7790

❼ Burlington Trail

Endpoints: Burlington to Rochester
Location: Racine County
Length: 4.0 miles
Surface: Crushed stone and gravel

Contact:
Tom Statz, Director
Park Planning & Program
Racine County Public Works Department
14200 Washington Avenue
Sturtevant, WI 53177-1253
(414)886-8440

❽ Cat Tail Trail

Endpoints: Almena to Amery
Location: Barron and Polk Counties
Length: 17.8 miles (will be 28.9 miles when completed)
Surface: Gravel

Contact:
Polk County
Information Center
710 Highway 35 South
St. Croix Falls, WI 54024
(800)222-7655

❾ Cheese Country Recreation Trail

Endpoints: Mineral Point to Monroe
Location: Green, Iowa, Lafayette Counties
Length: 57.0 miles
Surface: Crushed stone

Contact:
Stephen Hubner
Trail Coordinator
Tri-County Trail Commission
627 Washington Street
Darlington, WI 53530
(608)776-4830

❿ Chippewa River State Trail

Endpoints: Eau Claire to Caryville
Location: Dunn and Eau Claire Counties
Length: 18.0 miles
Surface: Asphalt

Contact:
Jean Rygiel
Trails Coordinator
Wisconsin DNR
Western Division
1300 West Clairmont Avenue
P.O. Box 4001
Eau Claire, WI 54701-6127
(715)839-1607

⑪ Clover Creek Trail

Endpoints: Chequamegon National Forest
Location: Price County
Length: 2.5 miles of 15.8-mile trail is on abandoned rail corridor
Surface: Grass and dirt

Contact:
Victor W. Peterson
Forestry Technician
Chequamegon National Forest
1170 South 4th Avenue
Park Falls, WI 54552
(715)762-2461

⑫ Elroy–Sparta State Park Trail

Endpoints: Elroy to Sparta
Location: Juneau and Monroe Counties
Length: 32.0 miles
Surface: Crushed stone

Contact:
Ron Nelson, Superintendent
Wildcat Work Unit
P.O. Box 99
Ontario, WI 54651-0099
(608)337-4775

⑬ Florence County Snowmobile Trail

Endpoints: Nicolet National Forest
Location: Florence County
Length: 4.0 miles of 32.4-mile trail is on abandoned rail corridor
Surface: Gravel and dirt

Contact:
Dave Poquette
Assistant Ranger
Nicolet National Forest
USFS - Florence Ranger District
HC 1, Box 83
Florence, WI 54121
(715)528-4464

⑭ Fort Atkinson to Koshkonong Trail

Endpoints: Fort Atkinson to Koshkonong
Location: Jefferson County
Length: 3.0 miles of 4.0-mile trail is on abandoned rail corridor
Surface: Asphalt and crushed stone

Contact:
Joe Nehmer, Director
Jefferson County Parks Dept.
Courthouse
320 South Main Street
Jefferson, WI 53549
(414)674-7260

⑮ Gandy Dancer Trail

Location: Burnett, Douglas and Polk Counties
Length: 69.0 miles open in three separate sections

Burnett County Section
Endpoints: Danbury to Siren
Length: 20.0 miles
Surface: Original ballast

Contact:
Mike Luedeke
Forest Administrator
Burnett County Forest and Parks Department
7410 County Highway K
Siren, WI 54872-0106
(715)349-2157

Douglas County Section
Endpoints: Superior to Wisconsin state line
Length: 13.0 miles of 19.0-mile trail is on abandoned rail corridor
Surface: Original ballast

Contact:
Mark Schroeder
Douglas County Section
Resource & Rec. Manager
Douglas County Forestry Department
P.O. Box 211
Solon Springs, WI 54873
(715)378-2219

Polk County Section
Endpoints: St. Croix Falls to Polk County line
Length: 30.0 miles
Surface: Crushed stone

Contacts:
Polk County
Information Center
710 Highway 35 South
St. Croix Falls, WI 54024
(800)222-7655

Robert Wilson, Director
Polk County Parks Dept.
P.O. Box 623
Balsam Lake, WI 54810
(715)485-9272

⑯ Glacial Drumlin State Park Trail

Endpoints: Cottage Grove to Waukesha
Location: Dane, Jefferson and Waukesha Counties
Length: 47.2 miles of 48.6-mile trail is on abandoned rail corridor
Surface: Crushed stone

Eastern Section

Contact:
Paul Sandgren
Park Manager
Glacial Drumlin
State Park Trail
N846 W329/DNR-Lapham
Peak Unit-KMSF
C.T.H. Co. "C"
Delafield, WI 53018
(414)646-3025

Western Section

Contact:
Dana White, Park Manager
Glacial Drumlin
State Park Trail
Wisconsin Department of Natural Resources
1213 S. Main Street
Lake Mills, WI 53551-1818
(414)648-8774

⑰ Great River State Park Trail

Endpoints: Onalaska to Trempealeau National Wildlife Refuge
Location: Buffalo, La Crosse and Trempealeau Counties
Length: 22.0 miles of 24.0-mile trail is on abandoned rail corridor
Surface: Crushed stone

Contact:
Lois Isaacson
Perrot State Park
P.O. Box 407
Trempealeau, WI 54661
(608)534-6409

⑱ Hiawatha Trail

Endpoints: Tomahawk to Sara Park
Location: Lincoln County
Length: 6.6 miles (will be 10.6 miles when completed)
Surface: Crushed stone

Contact:
William Wengeler
County Forestry Administrator
Lincoln County Forestry Land and Parks
Courthouse Building
Merril, WI 54452
(715)536-0327

⑲ Hillsboro Trail

Endpoints: Hillsboro to Union Center
Location: Juneau County
Length: 4.3 miles
Surface: Crushed stone

Contact:
Dale Dorow, Administrator
Juneau County Forest and Parks Department
250 Oak Street
Mauston, WI 53948
(608)847-9390

⑳ Ice Age Trail

Endpoints: Langlade County Forest
Location: Langlade County
Length: 7.0 miles of 18.4-mile trail is on abandoned rail corridor
Surface: Gravel and original ballast

Contact:
Michael Sohasky
County Forest Admin.
Langlade County Forestry Department
P.O. Box 460
Antigo, WI 54409-0460
(715)627-6236

㉑ Iron Horse Trail

Endpoints: Manitowish to Frontier Campground
Location: Iron County
Length: 55.0 miles
Surface: Gravel

Contact:
Tom Salzmann
Administrator
Iron County Forestry Office
603 Third Avenue
Hurley, WI 54537
(715)561-2697

㉒ Kenosha County Bike Trail

Endpoints: Racine county line to Illinois state line
Location: Kenosha County
Length: 8.2 miles of 14.2-mile trail is on abandoned rail corridor
Surface: Asphalt and crushed stone

Contact:
Ric Ladine
Director of Parks
Kenosha County Parks
P.O. Box 549
Kenosha, WI 53104-0549
(414)857-1862

㉓ Kimball Creek Trail

Endpoints: Nicolet National Forest
Location: Forest County
Length: 10.0 miles of 12.0-mile trail is on abandoned rail corridor
Surface: Original ballast with parallel dirt treadway

Contact:
Bill Reardon
Forestry Technician
Nicolet National Forest
Eagle River Ranger District
P.O. Box 1809
Eagle River, WI 54521
(715)479-2827

㉔ La Crosse River State Park Trail

Endpoints: Sparta to La Crosse
Location: La Crosse and Monroe Counties
Length: 21.5 miles
Surface: Crushed stone

Contact:
Ron Nelson, Superintendent
Wildcat Work Unit
P.O. Box 99
Ontario, WI 54651-0099
(608)337-4775

㉕ Lake Country Trail

Endpoints: Delafield to Waukesha
Location: Waukesha County
Length: 6.5 miles of 8.0-mile trail is on abandoned rail corridor
Surface: Asphalt and crushed stone

Contact:
David Burch
Senior Landscape Architect
Waukesha County Parks
and Planning Commission
1320 Pewaukee Road
Waukesha, WI 53188
(414)548-7790

㉖ MRK Trail

Endpoints: Racine to Caledonia
Location: Racine County
Length: 5.0 miles
Surface: Crushed stone, gravel and original ballast

Contact:
Tom Statz, Director
Park Planning & Program
Racine County Public
Works Department
14200 Washington Avenue
Sturtevant, WI 53177-1253
(414)886-8440

㉗ Military Ridge State Park Trail

Endpoints: Dodgeville to Fitchburg
Location: Dane and Iowa Counties
Length: 39.6 miles
Surface: Crushed stone

Contact:
Gregory Pittz, Trail Manager
Military Ridge State Park Trail
4175 State Highway 23
Dodgeville, WI 53533-9506
(608)935-5119

㉘ New Berlin Trail

Endpoints: Waukesha to West Allis
Location: Waukesha County
Length: 6.0 miles
Surface: Crushed stone

Contact:
David Burch
Senior Landscape Architect
Waukesha County Parks
and Planning Commission
1320 Pewaukee Road
Waukesha, WI 53188
(414)548-7790

㉙ North Flambeau Cycle Trail

Endpoints: Chequamegon National Forest
Location: Price County
Length: 1.0 mile of 23.0-mile trail is on abandoned rail corridor
Surface: Dirt

Contact:
Victor Peterson
Forestry Technician
Chequamegon National Forest
1170 4th Avenue South
Park Falls, WI 54552
(715)762-2461

㉚ North Shore Trail

Endpoints: Racine to Kenosha County line
Location: Racine County
Length: 3.0 miles (will be 8.0 miles when completed)
Surface: Crushed stone and gravel

Contact:
Tom Statz, Director
Park Planning & Programs
Racine County Public
Works Department
14200 Washington Avenue
Sturtevant, WI 53177-1253
(414)886-8440

㉛ Old Abe Trail

Endpoints: Chippewa Falls to Cornell
Location: Chippewa County
Length: 17.0 miles
Surface: Original ballast

Contact:
Jean Rygiel
Trails Coordinator
Wisconsin DNR
Western Division
1300 West Clairmont Avenue
P.O. Box 4001
Eau Claire, WI 54701-6127
(715)839-1607

㉜ Oliver–Wrenshall Trail

Endpoints: Oliver to Wrenshall
Location: Douglas County
Length: 6.0 miles of 12.0-mile trail is on abandoned rail corridor
Surface: Grass and dirt

Contact:
David Epperly
or Mark Schroeder
Douglas County Forestry
Department
P.O. Box 211
Solon Springs, WI 54873
(715)378-2219

㉝ Omaha Trail

Endpoints: Camp Douglas to Elroy
Location: Juneau County
Length: 12.5 miles
Surface: Asphalt and gravel

Contact:
Dale Dorow, Administrator
250 Oak Street
Mauston, WI 53948
(608)847-9389

34 Pecatonica State Park Trail

Endpoints: Calamine to Belmont
Location: Grant and Lafayette Counties
Length: 11 miles (will be 18 miles when completed)
Surface: Crushed stone

Contact:
Stephen Hubner
Trail Coordinator
Tri-County Trail Commission
627 Washington Street
Darlington, WI 53530
(608)776-4830

35 Pine Line

Endpoints: Medford to Prentice
Location: Price and Taylor Counties
Length: 26.2 miles
Surface: Crushed stone and gravel

Price County Section
Contact:
Price County Tourism Office
126 Cherry Street
Phillips, WI 54555
(800)269-4505

Taylor County Section
Contact:
Taylor County Tourism Council
224 South Second Street
Medford, WI 54451
(800)257-4729

36 Red Cedar State Trail

Endpoints: Menomonie to Dunnville
Location: Dunn County
Length: 14.5 miles
Surface: Crushed stone

Contact:
James Janowak, Manager
Red Cedar State Trail
921 Brickyard Road
Menomonie, WI 54751-9100
(715)232-1242

37 Riley Lake Snowmobile Trail

Endpoints: Chequamegon National Forest
Location: Price County
Length: 7.8 miles of 23.0-mile trail is on abandoned rail corridor
Surface: Dirt and grass

Contact:
Victor Peterson
Forestry Technician
Chequamegon National Forest
1170 Fourth Avenue South
Park Falls, WI 54552
(715)762-2461

38 Rush Lake Trail

Endpoints: Berlin to Ripon
Location: Winnebago County
Length: 5.3 miles
Surface: Original ballast

Contact:
Jeffrey A. Christensen
Parks Director
Winnebago County Parks
500 E. County Road Y
Oshkosh, WI 54901
(414)424-0042

39 Sugar River State Park Trail

Endpoints: New Glarus to Brodhead
Location: Green County
Length: 23.0 miles
Surface: Crushed stone

Contact:
Reynold Zeller
Superintendent
Sugar River State Park Trail
P.O. Box 781
New Glarus, WI 53574-0781
(608)527-2334

40 The "400" State Trail

Endpoints: Elroy to Reedsburg
Location: Juneau and Sauk Counties
Length: 22.0 miles
Surface: Crushed stone with parallel grass treadway

Contacts:
Ron Nelson, Superintendent
Wildcat Work Unit
P.O. Box 99
Ontario, WI 54651-0099
(608)337-4775

Jerry Trumm
Superintendent
Mirror Lake State Park
E10320 Fern Dell Road
Baraboo, WI 53913-9341
(608)254-2333

41 Tri-County Corridor

Endpoints: Ashland to Superior
Location: Ashland, Bayfield and Douglas Counties
Length: 61.8 miles
Surface: Asphalt and original ballast

 on certain sections

Contact:
Richard Mackey
P.O. Box 503
Ashland, WI 54806
(715)682-5299

42 Tuscobia State Trail

Endpoints: Park Falls to Rice Lake
Location: Barron, Price, Sawyer and Washburn Counties
Length: 73.0 miles of 74.0-mile trail is on abandoned rail corridor
Surface: Gravel, original ballast and grass

Contact:
Raymond Larsen
Superintendent
Tuscobia State Park Trail
Route 2, Box 2003
Hayward, WI 54843
(715)634-6513

43 Waterford–Wind Lake Trail

Endpoints: Waterford to Wind Lake
Location: Racine County
Length: 5.0 miles
Surface: Crushed stone and gravel

Contact:
Tom Statz, Director
Park Planning & Program
Racine County Public Works Department
14200 Washington Avenue
Sturtevant, WI 53177-1253
(414)886-8440

44 Waukesha Bike Trails

Endpoints: Waukesha
Location: Waukesha County
Length: 2.0 miles of 2.5-mile trail is on abandoned rail corridor
Surface: Asphalt and crushed stone

Contact:
David Kopp, City Planner
Waukesha City Planning, Room 200
201 Delafield Street
Waukesha, WI 53188-3690
(414)524-3752

45 Wild Goose State Trail

Endpoints: Clyman Junction to Fond du Lac
Location: Dodge and Fond du Lac Counties
Length: 34.0 miles of 34.0-mile trail is on abandoned rail corridor
Surface: Crushed stone

Dodge County Section

Contact:
David Carpenter
Executive Director
Dodge County Planning & Development Department
Administrative Building
Juneau, WI 53039
(414)386-3700

Fond du Lac County Section

Contact:
Wayne Rollin or Sam Tobias
Fond du Lac County Planning & Parks Dept.
160 South Macy Street
Fond du Lac, WI 54935-4241
(414)929-3135

46 Wiouwash Trail

Endpoints: Hortonville to Oshkosh
Location: Outagamie and Winnebago Counties
Length: 20.3 miles
Surface: Crushed stone and original ballast

Outagamie County Section

Contact:
Christopher Brandt
Director
Outagamie County Parks
1375 East Broadway Drive
Appleton, WI 54915
(414)832-4790

Winnebago County Section

Contact:
Jeffrey Christensen
Director
Winnebago County Department of Parks
500 East County Road Y
Oshkosh, WI 54901
(414)424-0042

47 Woodville Trail

Endpoints: Woodville to St. Croix County line
Location: St. Croix County
Length: 7.0 miles
Surface: Gravel and dirt

Contacts:
Sue Nelson, County Clerk
Government Center
1101 Carmichael Road
Hudson, WI 54016
(715)386-4600

Allen Stene, Chairman
Woodville Trail Committee
210 South Main Street
P.O. Box 302
Woodville, WI 54028-9546
(715)698-2401

WYOMING

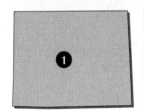

1 Wyoming Heritage Trail

Endpoints: Riverton to Shoshoni
Location: Fremont County
Length: 22.0 miles
Surface: Asphalt and original ballast

Contact:
Mike Morgan
Executive Director
Fremont County Association of Governments
818 South Federal Boulevard
Riverton, WY 82501-4901
(307)857-3644

APPENDIX: STATE TRAIL PLANNERS

700 Great Rail-Trails offers a comprehensive listing of the nation's 700 trails built on abandoned rail corridors. However, if you are interested in finding additional off-road trails (not built on abandoned rail corridors), Rails-to-Trails Conservancy recommends that you contact the appropriate state trail planner. The following list includes contact information for the nation's 49 state trail planners.

Jon C. Strickland
Recreation Program Manager
Department of Economics
and Community Affairs
401 Adams Avenue
Montgomery, AL 36103
(205)242-5483

Ron Crenshaw
Department of Natural
Resources
Division of Parks and
Outdoor Recreation
3601 C Street, Suite 1200
Anchorage, AK 99503
(907)762-2613

Pam Gilmore
Arizona State Parks
1300 West Washington
Phoenix, AZ 85007
(602)542-7116

Ken Eastin
Arkansas State Parks
1 Capitol Mall
Little Rock, AR 72201
(501)682-1227

Charlie Willard
Department of Parks and
Recreation
Statewide Planning Section
P.O. Box 942896
Sacramento, CA 94296-0001
(916)653-8803

Stuart Macdonald
Division of Parks and
Outdoor Recreation
1313 Sherman Street,
Room 618
Denver, CO 80203
(303)866-3203 ext. 306

Joseph Hickey
Outdoor Recreation Planner
Department of
Environmental Protection
Bureau of Outdoor
Recreation
79 Elm Street
Hartford, CT 06106-5127
(203)424-3200

Jack Goins
Delaware Parks and
Recreation
P.O. Box 1401
Dover, DE 19903
(302)739-4413

Ted Pochter
Department of Recreation
and Parks
Office of Policy, Planning
and Evaluation
3149 Sixteenth Street, NW
Washington, DC 20010
(202)673-7692

Collier Clark
Department of
Environmental Protection
Bureau of Design and
Construction
Mail Station 520
3900 Commonwealth Blvd.
Tallahassee, FL 32399
(904)488-3538

Alicia R. Soriano
Department of Natural
Resources
Parks, Recreation and
Historic Sites Division
205 Butler Street
Suite 1352E
Atlanta, GA 30334
(404)656-6530

Ralston Nagata
State Parks Administrator
Division of State Parks and
Recreation
P.O. Box 621
Honolulu, HI 96809
(808)587-0300

Leo Hennesy
Department of Parks and
Recreation
P.O. Box 83720
Boise, ID 83720-0065
(208)334-4199

Bob Thornberry
Department of Natural
Resources
524 South Second Street,
Room 310
Springfield, IL 62701-1787
(217)782-3715

Tom Kidd
Department of Natural
Resources
Division of Outdoor
Recreation
402 West Washington,
Room 271
Indianapolis, IN 46204
(317)232-4070

Nancy J. Burns
Office of Project Planning
Iowa Department of
Transportation
800 Lincoln Way
Ames, IA 50010
(515)239-1621

Ed Alvis
Kansas Department of
Wildlife and Parks
P.O. Box 777
1500 West Seventh Street
Topeka, KS 66720
(316)431-0380

Carey Tichnor
Division of Recreation
Kentucky Department of
Parks
Capitol Plaza Tower
10th floor
500 Mero Street
Frankfort, KY 40601
(502)564-4940 ext. 246

Trail Planner
Department of Culture,
Recreation and Tourism
Division of Outdoor
Recreation
P.O. Box 44426
Baton Rouge, LA 70804
(504)342-8186

Tom Cieslinski
Bureau of Parks and
Recreation
State House, Station #22
Augusta, ME 04333
(207)287-4962

Theresa Moore
Greenways and Resource
Planning
Department of Natural
Resources
Tawes Office Building, D3
580 Taylor Avenue
Annapolis, MD 21401
(410)974-3589

**Jennifer Howard
Danny O'Brien**
Division of Resource
Conservation
Department of
Environmental Management
100 Cambridge Street
Saltonstall Building
Room 1404
Boston, MA 02202
(617)727-3160 ext. 557

Hector Chlunti
Department of Natural
Resources
Forest Management Division
P.O. Box 30028
Lansing, MI 48909
(517)335-3040

Laurie Young
Trails and Waterways Unit
Department of Natural
Resources
500 Lafayette Road
St. Paul, MN 55155-4052
612-296-6690

James Graves
Outdoor Recreation Grants
Division of Parks
Department of Wildlife,
Fisheries and Parks
P.O. Box 451
Jackson, MS 39205-0451
(601)364-2156

Deborah Schnack
Department of Natural
Resources
Division of State Parks
P.O. Box 176
Jefferson City, MO 65102
(314)751-5360

Bob Walker
Department of Fish,
Wildlife and Parks
Parks Division
1420 East Sixth Avenue
P.O. Box 200701
Helena, MT 59620-0701
(406)444-4585

Kathleen Foote
Game and Parks
Commission
2200 North 33rd Street
P.O. Box 30370
Lincoln, NE 68503
(402)471-5425

Steve Weaver
Chief
Planning and Development
Division of State Parks
123 West Nye Lane
Carson City, NV 89710
(702)687-4384

Paul Gray
Chief
Trails Bureau
Division of Parks and
Recreation
P.O. Box 1856
Concord, NH 03302
(603)271-3254

Celeste Tracy
Office of Natural Lands
Management
New Jersey Division of
Parks and Forestry
CN 404
Trenton, NJ 08625-0404
(609)984-1173

Robert Rhinehardt
Office of Parks, Recreation
and Historic Preservation
Agency Building Number 1
Empire State Plaza
17th floor
Albany, NY 12238
(518)486-2909

Darrell McBane
Division of Parks and
Recreation
12700 Bayleaf Road
Raleigh, NC 27614
(919)846-9991

Randy Harmon
Department of Parks and
Recreation
1835 East Bismark
Expressway
Bismarck, ND 58504
(701)328-5369

William Daehler
Department of Natural
Resources
Division of Real Estate and
Land Management
1952 Belcher, Building C-4
Columbus, OH 43224
(614)265-6402

Susan Henry
Oklahoma Tourism and
Recreation Department
Division of Planning and
Development
2401 North Lincoln
Suite 500
Oklahoma City, OK 73105
(405)521-2973

Peter Bond
Oregon State Parks and
Recreation Department
1115 Commercial Street NE
Salem, OR 97310-1001
(503)378-5012

Edwin Deaton
Rails-to-Trails Program
Manager
Department of Conservation
and Natural Resources
Bureau of State Parks
P.O. Box 8551
Harrisburg, PA 17105-8551
(717)787-6674

Ginny Leslie
Department of
Environmental Management
Division of Planning
and Development
83 Park Street
Providence, RI 02903
(401)277-2776

Marshal Johnson
Department of Parks,
Recreation and Tourism
Edgar Brown Building,
Suite 320
1205 Pendleton Street
Columbia, SC 29201
(803)734-0141

Kim Raap
Department of Game, Fish
and Parks
Foss Building
523 East Capital Avenue
Pierre, SD 57501
(605)773-3391

Bob Richards
Department of Environment
and Conservation
Division of Recreation
Services
L&C Tower, 10th floor
401 Church Street
Nashville, TN 37243-0439
(615)532-0753

Kathryn Nichols
Texas Parks and Wildlife
Department
Greenways Program
4200 Smith School Road
Austin, TX 78744
(512)389-4735

John Knudson
Department of Natural
Resources
Division of Parks and
Recreation
1636 West North Temple,
Suite 116
Salt Lake City, UT 84116
(801)538-7344

George Plumb
Director of Recreation
Department of Forests,
Parks and Recreation
103 South Main Street
Waterbury, VT 05676
(802)241-3655

Jim Eychaner
Interagency Committee for
Outdoor Recreation
P.O. Box 40917
Olympia, WA 98504-0917
(206)902-3000

**West Virginia Division
of Tourism**
2101 Washington Street, E.
Charleston, WV 25305
(304)558-2200

David Hammer
Department of Natural
Resources
Bureau of Parks and
Recreation
P.O. Box 7921
Madison, WI 53707
(608)264-6034

Trail Planner
Department of Commerce
Division of Parks and
Cultural Resources
2301 Central Avenue
Cheyenne, WY 82002
(307)777-7550